QSE
QUICK SMART ENGLISH

Pre-Intermediate
WORKBOOK

Rebecca Robb Benne

with

Joanne Collie

BROOKEMEAD ENGLISH LANGUAGE TEACHING

QSE
QUICK SMART ENGLISH
Pre-Intermediate
WORKBOOK

Series editor: Duncan Prowse
Contributor and consultant: Joanne Collie
Consultant: Rosemary Harris
Assistant editors: Deborah Friedland, Anna Kutz
Designer: John Anastasio

The QSE series makes a valuable contribution to preparation for Trinity's Graded Examinations in Spoken English and Integrated Skills Examinations

QSE Pre-Intermediate Workbook Common European Framework Level A2-B1

QSE Series Title	Common European Framework	UCLES	Michigan	TOEFL (New TOEFL)	Trinity College, London, ESOL	Edexcel London Test of English
Quick Start English	A1-A2	KET			ISE 0 GESE Grade 1, 2, 3	Level (A1) 1
Quick Smart English 1 Pre-Intermediate	A2-B1	PET	BCCE		ISE I, GESE Grade 4, 5, 6	Level 1-2
Quick Smart English 2 Intermediate	B1-B2	FCE	ECCE	450-525 Target 485 (NT 163)	ISE II, GESE Grade 7, 8, 9	Level 2-3
Quick Smart English 3 Advanced	B2-C1	CAE	ALCE	Target 525 (NT 197)	ISE III, GESE Grade 10, 11	Level 3-4

ISBN: 1-905248-09-1
978-1-905248-09-4

Also available:
QSE Pre-Intermediate Student's Book, ISBN 1-905248-08-3
QSE Pre-Intermediate CD 1 Listening and pronunciation, ISBN 1-905248-10-5
QSE Pre-Intermediate CD 2 Reading, ISBN 1-905248-11-3
QSE Pre-Intermediate Teacher's Guide, ISBN 1-905248-15-6

Other books in the QSE Series:
QSE Intermediate (CEF B1-B2)
Student's Book, Workbook, Audio CDs, Teacher's Guide
QSE Advanced (CEF B2-C1)
Student's Book and Workbook, Audio and DVD, Teacher's Guide

Published by
Brookemead English Language Teaching, London
© Brookemead Associates Ltd. 2006
All rights reserved. No part of this publication may be reproduced, recorded, transmitted, or stored in any form whatsoever, without the prior written permission of the copyright holders.

QSE Pre-Intermediate Workbook — CONTENTS

Unit	Title	Functions, Language Banks	Grammar	Pronunciation CD 1, track	Writing	Pages
1	Adrenalin rush	1 Talking about permanent situations and repeated actions 2 Talking about the past	The past simple/present simple, sequencing words		Email to a friend Article for magazine Letter to newspaper	4-5
2	Carnival atmosphere	3 Giving advice (should) 4 Describing frequency and manner	Adverbs of frequency and manner		Article for college magazine Email to penfriend Description of a concert	6-7
3	Lifestyle choices	5 Comparing two things, more than two things	Comparatives, superlatives of adjectives	❹ Vowels	Email to a friend Article for newspaper Description of job	8-9
4	Stranger than fiction	6 Expressing likes and dislikes 7 Talking about future plans and intentions	Going to future Gerunds	❻ Consonants	Email about plans Essay about likes and dislikes Article for magazine	10-11
5	Shopaholics	8 Complaining 9 Quantifying	Adverbials of quantity Quantifiers		Email about shopping Tips for shoppers Description of dream shop	12-13
6	Eat your greens!	10 Asking for and giving reasons 11 Making and replying to requests	Connecting words: and, but, because	❾ Word stress	Email to a friend Report on food Story about food	14-15
7	For your eyes only	12 Talking about events in the indefinite or recent past	Present perfect with ever, never, just	⓫ Strong and weak forms	Email to a friend Essay about privacy Description of internet use	16-17
8	Fashionistas	13 Talking on the phone 14 Expressing preferences	Articles		Letter to a friend Description of clothes Story of life of a designer	18-19
	Progress check 1					20-21
9	Rule of law	15 Expressing obligation and necessity	Modals of obligation and necessity: must, have to, need to	⓮ Stress on auxiliary verbs	Article about communes Letter of comment Essay on rules	22-23
10	What's next?	16 Giving and following instructions 17 Informing about and predicting the future	will future for predictions		Email about a gadget Easy about the future Description of invention	24-25
11	Travel costs	18 Asking about and stating the duration of events	Present perfect with for and since	⓱ Consonant clusters 1	Letter about a holiday Article about the environment Description of transport types	26-27
12	Money, money, money	19 Using telephone banking 20 Expressing certainty and uncertainty	Modals: will and might Too, enough		Email to a friend Article about money Story about you and money	28-29
13	Destination disaster	21 Expressing intention and purpose	Infinitive of purpose Order of adjectives	⓴ Consonant clusters 2	Letter about cycling Article about cars Story about an accident	30-31
14	All in the family	22 Asking about and describing past activities 23 Asking about and describing events	Past continuous	㉒ Intonation in statements	Email about your family Essay about family life Description of special occasion	32-33
15	The new epidemics	24 Talking about facts 25 Requesting and expressing opinions and impressions	Zero and first conditionals		Email to a hypochondriac Article about disease Essay on smoking	34-35
16	Adventures in language	26 Making arrangements 27 Talking about future arrangements and intentions	Present continuous for future arrangements	㉕ Intonation in questions	Email about plans for the weekend Tips for students of English	36-37
	Progress check 2					38-39
	Language banks and exercises					40-48
	Audio texts					49-57
	Unit-by-unit word lists					58-65

Unit 1 Adrenalin rush — Workbook

See pages 8–11

1 Language: the present simple and past simple

Use the present simple to talk about:	
Things that are permanent and don't change:	**Things that happen many times, a routine:**
• My memories **stay** with me all the time.	• I always **wear** a helmet when I go skateboarding.

Use the past simple to talk about events that happened at one specific time in the past:
- I first **tried** surfing in 1999. (The time is mentioned.)
- My friend **gave** me a surfboard. (One specific event. No time is mentioned.)

We form the past simple of regular verbs with -ed. Somtimes the spelling of the verb changes.
- I **tried** inline skating yesterday. • I **injured** my knee. • I **stopped** skating.

We form simple present negatives and questions with *do*. In the same way, we form simple past negatives and questions with *did*.
- When **did she start** surfing? • She **didn't enjoy** surfing.

A Read the questions. Complete the ⊕ positive and ⊖ negative answers.

Example: Did your Mum worry? ⊕ Yes, she worried at first. ⊖ No, she didn't worry at all.

1 Did she think it was dangerous? a) Yes, she ….. it was. b) No, she ….. ….. it was.
2 When did you start skating? a) I ….. at five. b) I ….. ….. until I was 10.
3 Did you get scared? a) I ….. scared at first. b) Later, I ….. scared at all.
4 Did you wear your helmet? a) Yes, I always ….. it. b) No, I ….. ….. it.
5 Did you have fun? a) Yes, I ….. a lot of fun. b) I ….. ….. any fun at all!

B Jane interviews Helga Holt, motocross rider. Put the verbs in the right tense.

Jane Hi Helga. How did you get into riding motocross bikes?
Helga A friend of mine suggested I try it. So I (1 *buy*) ….. a motocross bike and (2 *start*) ….. riding. I (3 *try*) ….. jumping because my friend (4 *say*) ….. there were no girls doing it.
Jane Do you get scared when you're flying off a big jump?
Helga I (5 *be*) ….. scared, when I first started. But I'm not scared now. I always (6 *feel*) ….. really excited
Jane What was your worst injury?
Helga Once I (7 *crack*) ….. my ribs, and I (8 *sprain*) ….. my wrist.
Jane Why do you do it?
Helga It's cool. I (9 *love*) ….. the adrenalin rush. And can you believe it? Now somebody (10 *pay*) ….. me to ride my bike. I'm lucky.

C Answer these interview questions about you.
1 What sport do you do? ……………………………………………………………………
2 When did you start doing it? ……………………………………………………………
3 Do you ever get sports injuries? ………………………………………………………
4 Why do you do it? …………………………………………………………………………

Adrenalin rush Workbook

2 Vocabulary

A Find two more words for each list.

Sports that need wheels	• biking
Sports that use balls	• basketball
Sports that are in water	• swimming
Sports injuries	• cuts

B Put the sentences in the right order. Use the sequencing words to complete them.

| First | Then | Next |
| The next minute | | Finally |

First we put on our protective suits, helmet and goggles.
☐ …... I was out in the air, flying.
☐ …... we got into the plane and took off.
☐ …... I landed safely.
☐ …... I stood at the open door, feeling scared.

C Complete the sentences with the correct words from the box.

| a) bandage | b) great | c) elevated |
| d) dangerous | e) scared | |

1 The coach gives ………… advice!
2 My parents definitely think the sport's ………… .
3 Keep an injured leg ………… .
4 Wrap a ………… around the knee to support it.
5 I'm ………… when I'm flying off a big jump.

3 Word Building

A Complete the table. All the missing words are in Unit 1.

Nouns	Adjectives
tradition	1
2	protective
sport	3
sprain	4
5	thrilling
relaxation	6
7	dangerous
injury	8

4 Use of English

A Complete the second sentence so that it means the same as the first.

1 Football isn't interesting.
   Football is ………. .
2 It's danger that makes this sport so thrilling.
   This sport is thrilling because it's ………… .
3 I hated the sport.
   I ……… *like the sport*.
4 Don't stand on your sprained ankle.
   ………… *your sprained ankle*.
5 Don't let your injured friend get cold.
   Keep your injured friend ………… .

5 Portfolio Writing

A Your friend sends you an email to say she wants to go motocross riding. Write her a reply and say why this is a good or a bad idea (70–80 words).

B Write an article for your school or sports club magazine about first aid for sports injuries (120–150 words).

C Write a letter to your local newspaper to explain why you think it's a good (or a bad) idea to do traditional sports rather than extreme sports (120–150 words).

Unit 2 Carnival atmosphere — Workbook — See pages 12–15

1 Language: adverbs of frequency and manner

Adverbs of frequency express *how often* we do something:

100%
- always
- almost always
- usually
- often
- sometimes
- occasionally
- hardly ever
0%
- never

Adverbs of frequency go:
– *between* the subject and the verb:
- We **always** have a good time.

– but *after* the verb to be:
- He is **never** happy.

– and *between* the auxiliary and main verb:
- They don't **often** go to clubs.

A How often do you do these things? Write sentences with adverbs of frequency.

1 Listen to music. ....
2 Listen to songs in a foreign language. ....
3 Watch music TV. ....
4 Go to concerts or music festivals. ....
5 Sing in a group. ....
6 Sing in the shower or bath. ....

Adverbs of manner express *how* we do something:
- He plays the drums **madly**.

Adverb formation = adjective +*ly*
- traditional → traditionally
- angry → angrily

Learn these irregular adverbs:
- good → well
- hard → hard
- fast → fast
- late → late

Adverbs of manner go *after* the verb. If the verb has an object, the adverb goes after the object.
- She sings **well**.
- She sings that song **well**.

B Complete the sentences. Use the adjectives in the box to make adverbs.

a) uncomfortable	b) hungry	c) tired	d) happy	e) worried

1 "This is a fantastic carnival," she said ..... .
2 "My costume is a bit hot," she said ..... .
3 "Let's get some food," he said ..... .
4 "Oh, no! I can't find my money," she said ..... .
5 "I need to get some sleep," he said ..... .

C Write three or four sentences about one of your free time activities. How often do you do this activity? How well can you do it?

Carnival atmosphere — Workbook

Unit 2

2 Vocabulary

A Complete the text with the correct words from the box.

a) controversial	b) good time	c) carnival
d) parade	e) costumes	f) protests
g) festival	h) floats	i) music

In Germany, (1) …… is a tradition that began before Christianity. It was a (2) …… to celebrate the end of winter. Today the (3) …… carry people wearing brightly coloured (4) …… through the streets. There is lots of noise and (5) ……. The biggest (6) …… is through the streets of Mainz. Traditionally, people use the carnival to make (7) …… about local politicians and there are many (8) …… speeches. But for most people, the main idea of carnival is to have a (9) …….

B Put the words from the box in the correct lists.

amp	beat	sound	headphones
vocal	mixer	deck	scratches
cables	speaker		

DJ equipment	Parts of a song
• amp	• beat

C Add more musical instruments to each list.

Instruments you play with your hands	Instruments you play with your mouth
• keyboard	• trumpet

3 Connections

A Find the correct preposition for each group.

1. a tradition / sponsorship / to be proud ☐ carnival / festivals / achievements
2. mix one track / change / be angry ☐ another / the times / somebody
3. complain / protest / be worried ☐ changes / corruption / violence

4 Use of English

A Complete the second sentence so that it means the same as the first.
1. There's a famous carnival in Rio de Janeiro.
   Rio de Janeiro ……… a famous carnival.
2. The Samba Parade in Rio is huge.
   The Samba Parade in Rio is ………big.
3. I thought the atmosphere was fantastic.
   I ………… the atmosphere.
4. The people in the parade were very good dancers.
   The people in the parade danced ………
5. I didn't remember to take my camera.
   I ……… to take my camera.

5 Portfolio Writing

A Write an article for your college magazine. Explain why you think traditional celebrations are important or not (120–150 words).

B Write an email to a penfriend. Invite him/her to a carnival or festival in your country. Tell him/her what usually happens (70–80 words).

C Write a description of a concert or a club night you have enjoyed (120–150 words).

Unit 3 Lifestyle choices — Workbook

See pages 16–19

1 Language: comparatives and superlatives

Use comparatives to compare two things:	Use superlatives to compare more than two things:
• Skiing is **healthier** than watching TV. • It's **more** interesting and **less** stressful.	• This is the **healthiest** place in the world. • This is the **least** interesting lesson today.

One-syllable adjectives have comparatives ending in *-er* and superlatives ending in *-est*		
• small	• smaller	• smallest
Some two-syllable adjectives use *–er* and *–est*		
• risky	• riskier	• riskiest
Other two-syllable adjectives use *more / less* and *most / least*		
• secure	• more / less secure	• most / least secure
Longer adjectives use *more / less* and *most / least*		
• interesting	• more / less interesting	• most / least interesting
• beautiful	• more / less beautiful	• most / least beautiful

Irregular comparatives and superlatives:		
• good	• better	• best
• bad	• worse	• worst

A Complete the sentences. Use the correct form of the adjectives in brackets.

1 Working outdoors is ………… than working indoors, but some people think it's ………… . (*healthy, boring*)
2 Managing a small hotel is ………… than being a cleaner, but owning a big hotel is ………… job of all. (*hard*)
3 Working in a financial organisation is ………… than working for yourself, but many young people think it's ………… . (*secure, interesting*)
4 Meetings can be the ………… way to motivate people, but the ………… thing about them is that they waste a lot of time. (*good, bad*)

B Highlight the mistakes and write in the correct comparisons or superlatives.

Reporter	What is the most good thing about your college, Shaun?	1 …………
Shaun	Well, the head of our college wants students to make decisions and that's most democratic than schools where the teachers make all the decisions.	2 …………
Reporter	Does that mean having a lot of most boring thing of all – meetings?	3 …………
Shaun	In business studies, we learn how to have effecter meetings.	4 …………
	For example, we read the agenda, so we're all careful now than we were before. We only ask importantest questions.	5 ………… 6 …………

C Write three or four sentences to compare a job you like with a job you don't like.

Unit 3
Lifestyle choices — Workbook

2 Vocabulary

A Put the expressions into the correct categories for you. Add other expressions to each category.

| secure | stressful | time for other activities |
| friendly | money | challenging | hours |

Working ...	Good things	Bad things
1 as a sole trader		
2 in a partnership		
3 in a large company		

B Complete the definitions.
1. A person who writes software is a ....
2. Money paid regularly to a person who works for a company is a ....
3. Moving up to a better job in a company is a ....
4. A list of topics to discuss at a meeting is an ....

3 Use of English

A Complete the second sentence so that it means the same as the first.

1. A sole trader is less secure than an employee in a large company.
   Working for a large company is .... than being a sole trader.
2. Setting up their own business is a goal for many young people.
   Many young people want .... their own business.
3. There is nowhere that has a cleaner environment than the Alps.
   The Alps has .... environment in the world.
4. It's bad to arrive late for a meeting.
   It's good to arrive .... for a meeting.

4 Pronunciation: Vowels

A Some vowel sounds in English can have different spellings.
Listen to these examples.

| ship (1) | sheep (2) | get (3) |

Mark the vowel sounds of these words with the correct number:
a) friend ☐   b) ski ☐
c) instructor ☐ d) teach ☐
e) winter ☐   f) spends ☐
g) cleaner ☐   h) healthier ☐
i) environment ☐ j) centre ☐
k) specialist ☐ l) business ☐
m) meeting ☐   n) people ☐
o) routine ☐

B Now listen to the sentences and check the answers you gave in A.

- My friend's a ski instructor – he teaches winter sports and spends his life in a cleaner and healthier environment.
- The garden centre specialist likes having her own business, meeting people, and not having a routine.

5 Portfolio Writing

A Your friend asks you for some ideas about organising meetings for the college music festival committee. Write an email to him or her (70–80 words).

B The government in England is trying to get more people to become teachers. Write an article for your school newspaper comparing teaching to another job that you think is more (or less) interesting (120–150 words).

C Describe your ideal job. Think about hours, salary, security, contact with people (120–150 words).

9

Unit 4 **Stranger than fiction** **Workbook** See pages 20–23

1 Language: *going to* future

> Use the *going to* future to talk about future plans and intentions.
> • I'm **going to watch** a DVD at home tomorrow.

> Form the *going to* future like this:
> **be + (not) going to + infinitive**
> • Are you **going to watch** *I Wanna Be a Star* this evening?
> • We're **not going to watch** TV.
> • We're **going to go** to a club.

> You can use these time expressions with the *going to* future.
> • This afternoon / evening
> • Tomorrow morning / afternoon / evening
> • On Saturday / Sunday / … .
> • At the weekend
> • Next week / month / year

A Complete the dialogue. Use the correct form of the *going to* future.

Emma	When (1 *we / see*) …… the new Tom Hanks film? Lucy says it's great. She (2 *watch*) …… it again at the weekend.
Rick	I (3 *not see*) …… that. You know I don't like Tom Hanks.
Emma	What about tomorrow? (4 *you / do*) …… then? I (5 *not do*) …… anything.
Rick	Ali (6 *come*) …… here tomorrow. We (7 *not see*) …… that film, Emma, OK!
Emma	Fine. And I (8 *not go*) ….. to the concert with you on Saturday.
Rick	What? Oh, alright. What about Friday?

Gerunds

> Gerunds are verb forms, but we use them like nouns. They can be the subject or object of a sentence, or follow prepositions.
> • **Watching** TV is my favourite activity.
> • I love **going** to the cinema.
> • I'm interested in **studying** film.
> • I'm good at **making** video films.

> We make gerunds like like this: **verb + -ing**
> • watch ➔ • watching; write ➔ • writing; stop ➔ • stopping; lie ➔ • lying

B Complete these sentences about you.

1 …… is my favourite activity.
2 I love ……
3 I'm interested in ……
4 I'm good at ……

2 Use of English

A Complete the second sentence so that it means the same as the first.

1 I don't like watching TV.
   I'm not …… on watching TV.
2 Reality TV doesn't harm anyone.
   Reality TV is …… .
3 Nothing is worse than that show.
   That show is the …… show in the world.
4 I watch *Survivor* every week.
   I …… watch *Survivor*.
5 I like game shows the most.
   Game shows are my …… programmes.

Stranger than fiction Workbook

Unit 4

3 Vocabulary

A Match the TV programmes with the correct words from the box.

| a) documentary | b) game show |
| c) news | d) soap opera | e) talk show |

1 All the stories from around the world with Beth Lane.
2 Jay's guests tonight include pop star Toni Guy and actress Belle DeVere.
3 Who will win the $1 million prize this evening?
4 The Garcia family copes with the death of baby Louis.
5 A look at the life of lions in African game parks.

B Read the texts in Unit 4 again. Find the American words and spellings.

1 **British**   **American words**
   a) disgusting   ....
   b) stupid   ....
   c) they're terrible   ....
   d) mum   ....
   e) film   ....

2 **British spelling**   **American spelling**
   a) programme*   ....
   b) favourite   ....
   c) trivialise   ....
   d) neighbour   ....
   e) colour   ....

* a program in British English is a computer program

C Complete the text with the correct words from the box.

| a) cast | b) continuity | c) crew | d) location |
| e) plot | f) scene | g) shooting schedule |

The *Lord of the Rings: Return of the King* with its (1) ... of stars won eleven Oscars in 2004. The director shot the film on (2) ... in New Zealand with a (3) ... of sixteen months. The (4) ... filmed the (5) ... from all three *Lord of the Rings* films at the same time. *Return of the King* also has a complicated (6) ... so it's not surprising that there were problems of (7) ... . One website lists 172 errors for the film!

4 Pronunciation: Consonants

Some pairs of English consonants sound similar, but one is *voiceless* and another is *voiced*.

A1 Listen to these pairs of words. Can you hear the difference?

voiceless	voiced
fewer	viewer
came	game

2 Repeat the word pairs. Hold your throat – can you *feel* the difference? *Voiced* means that you use the vocal chords in your throat. *Voiceless* means that you don't use your vocal chords to pronounce the word.

Look at the word pairs below.

B1 Listen and circle the word you hear.

	voiceless	voiced
a)	Ted	dead
b)	ferry	very
c)	sink	zinc
d)	Pitt	bit
e)	class	glass
f)	choke	joke

2 Listen again and check your answers.
3 Repeat the pairs of words.

5 Portfolio Writing

A Write an email to a friend and tell him/her about your plans for the week. Ask your friend what his/her plans are (70–80 words). Use *going to*.

B Write a short essay (120–150 words). What sort of films do you like and dislike? Why? Give examples.

C Is reality TV good TV? Write an article for your college magazine. First explain what reality TV is. Then discuss the good and bad points. Finally, say if you think reality TV is good TV (120–150 words).

Unit 5 **Shopaholics** **Workbook** See pages 24–27

1 Language: adverbials of quantity

| We use adverbials of quantity to say how much we do something.
[+ +] • a lot
[+] • a little
[–] • not much
[– –] • not at all | Adverbials of quantity usually go after the verb and the object.
• I don't enjoy shopping **at all**.
• I read **a lot**. |

A Write about Maria and Jimmy.

Maria
1 enjoy/spending money   [+ +]
2 stay/at home   [–]
3 go out/with boy friends   [+ +]
4 watch/TV   [– –]
5 listen/to music   [+]

Jimmy
6   like/go out   [–]
7   play/computer games   [+ +]
8   read   [–]
9   enjoy/shopping   [– –]
10 shop/on the internet   [+]

1 • Maria enjoys spending money a lot.
2   She …
3
4
5

6 • Jimmy doesn't like going out much.
7   He …
8
9
10

| We use *how much* …? and *how many* …? to ask about quantity. |||
| We use *how much* with uncountable nouns.
• **How much** money have you got? | We use *how many* in questions with countable plural nouns.
• **How many** DVDs did you buy? |

Quantifiers

We use quantifiers to quantify nouns: [+ +] *a lot of / lots of* [+ +] *much / many* [+] *a little / a few*	
We use *a lot of / lots of* with countable and uncountable nouns.	• I've got **a lot of** money. • I've got **lots of** magazines.
We use *much* and *a little* with uncountable nouns.	• I haven't got **much** time. • I've got **a little** money.
We use *many* and *a few* with countable plural nouns.	• I haven't got **many** new things. • I've got **a few** T-shirts.
We usually use *much / many* in negative sentences, or in affirmative sentences with *so*.	• She's got **so many** clothes! • He's got **so much** money.

B Complete the dialogue with:

| how much | how many | a little | how much | a few | much | many | a lot of |

Ali You've got so (1) …. bags! (2) …. stuff have you bought, Sam?
Sam Well, I've got (3) ….. new clothes – all these here. And (4) …..CDs – not many, just three.
Ali Let's see. Wow! (5) …… T-shirts have you bought?
Sam Six. They were in the sale.
Ali Well, what about lunch? (6) ….. money have you got left?
Sam I've only got (7) ….. I think. No, I haven't got (8) ….. money left. Erm, can you lend me some, Ali?

12

Unit 5

Shopaholics Workbook

2 Vocabulary

A Complete the shopping crossword.

Across

3 Sales assistants sell things to them (9).
5 Women put their purse and lots of other things in this (7).
6 You buy food and other things here (11).
8 Your money back (6).
9 If you take something back to a shop, you need this (7).
11 You buy things to wear at this place (7, 4).
12 What the law says shoppers can do (8, 6).

Down

1 You can buy everything in this big shop (10, 5).
2 You can use it to buy things in a particular shop and pay the money later (5, 4).
4 It tells you what you have spent on your credit card (9).
7 A request to supply goods (5).
10 Money you keep in your purse or wallet (4).

3 Word building

Complete the tables with the correct words. All the missing words are in Unit 5.

Adjective	Noun	Verb	Noun
• angry	• anger	to explain	f) ………
a) ………	fault	to g) ………	criticism
private	b) ………	to pressurise	h) ………
c) ………	security	to i) ………	product
shocking	d) ………	to complain	j) ………
e) ………	use	to k) ………	cancellation

4 Use of English

A Complete the second sentence so that it means the same as the first.

1 It's too expensive.
   I can't …. it.
2 I only have a little time.
   I don't have ….. time.
3 The sales assistant wasn't polite to me.
   The sales assistant was ….. to me.
4 Can you please confirm my order?
   Can you please send me ….. of my order?
5 They hate shopping.
   They don't like shopping …….
6 I plan to go shopping later.
   I'm …… shopping later.

5 Portfolio Writing

A Write an email to a friend. Tell him or her about a shopping experience you had recently (70–80 words).

B Write an article for your college magazine with the title 'Tips for Shoppers' (120–150 words).

C Write a description of your dream shop. Write where it is, what it sells and why it is so great (120–150 words).

Unit 6 — Eat your greens! Workbook

See pages 28–31

1 Language: connecting words *and, but, because*

The connecting words *and*, *but* and *because* join together two main clauses.

and adds another positive or similar idea:	*but* adds a contrasting idea:	*because* adds a reason:
• I cook at home **and** I also eat out.	• He eats fish **but** he doesn't eat meat.	• I eat meat **because** I like it.

After *and* and *but* we can leave out the subject when the subject of both clauses is the same:
- We often eat out **and** (we) have a pizza.
- They like vegetables **but** (they) don't eat carrots.

A Join the sentences with *and*, *but* or *because*.

1 Many people are overweight ……………… they eat too much fat.
2 Chinese people eat rice ……………… British people prefer potatoes.
3 Australians eat crocodiles ……………… they like kangaroo meat, too.
4 In Europe dogs are pets ……………… in some countries they are a popular food.
5 In Tibet people put butter in tea ……………… they like the taste.

B Improve the paragraph. Rewrite it and add *and*, *but* or *because*.

My boyfriend and I went to a restaurant yesterday. We had a meal for his birthday. The restaurant was very busy. It was very noisy, too. My boyfriend wanted fish. There was no fish on the menu. So we had chicken. We both like that. It tasted okay. It wasn't anything special. The drinks were good. They were not very cold. We waited twenty minutes for the bill. Then we complained. We complained again when we got the bill. It was wrong. It wasn't a very good birthday!

C Complete the sentences about you.

1 I like ……………… and ………………
2 I hate ……………… but ………………
3 I don't eat ……………… because ………………
4 I eat ……………… because ………………

2 Use of English

A Complete the second sentence so that it means the same as the first.

1 My boyfriend is a quick eater.
   Example: • My boyfriend eats *quickly*.
2 Chocolate isn't as bad for you as fries.
   Fries are ……………… *for you than chocolate.*
3 We plan to eat out on Friday.
   We're ……………… *to eat out on Friday.*
4 There aren't a lot of vegetarians in the USA.
   There aren't ……………… *vegetarians in the USA.*
5 The food tasted horrible.
   The food ……………… *taste very good.*

Unit 6
Eat your greens! Workbook

3 Vocabulary

A Find the food items.

1	heesec	• cheese
2	steapoot	
3	siref	
4	bugiranee	
5	egrosan	
6	dearb	

B Write these numbers as figures (e.g. 123).

1	nine hundred and sixty-three	....
2	four thousand, three hundred and thirty-five	....
3	six hundred and seventy-two thousand	....
4	two hundred thousand, four hundred and fifty	....
5	one million, five hundred thousand	....

C Write these numbers as words:

1	841	....
2	78,615	....
3	157,000	....
4	999,987	....
5	3,760,203	....

D Complete the sentences with the correct words from the box.

a) calories	b) diet	c) fat	d) health
e) nutrients	f) weight		

1 You need lots of different foods in your ....
2 A lot of people count their ...... in their food and watch their ....
3 ...... and happiness are the important things in life.
4 Don't eat food with too much ...... or sugar.
5 ...... in food make you grow.

4 Pronunciation: Word stress

Word stress often changes in different forms of a word.

A1 Listen to and repeat these nouns and adjectives.

Noun	Adjective
environment	environmental
accident	accidental
misery	miserable
knowledge	knowledgeable
geography	geographic
economy	economic

2 Then listen again and underline the stressed syllable in each word.
3 In which words does the stress NOT change?

The nouns and verbs below have the same form but different stress.

B1 First listen and repeat.

Verb	Noun
produce	produce
increase	increase
decrease	decrease
export	export
research	research

2 Then listen again and underline the stressed syllable in each word.
3 Where is the stress on the nouns? Where is the stress on the verbs?

5 Portfolio Writing

A Your friend sends you an email saying she hasbecome a vegetarian. Write an email or a letter back and explain why you think this is a good or bad idea (70–80 words).

B Write a report for your college magazine about food which is typical of your region or country (120–150 words).

C Write a story describing your ideal meal: what food and drink, where, and who with (120–150 words). Start like this:

Unit 7 — For your eyes only — Workbook — See pages 66–69

1 Language: the present perfect with *ever, never, just*

Use the present perfect for actions that happened at an indefinite time in the past.
- I've **found** a great website.
- He's **checked** his email three times.

Use the present perfect + *ever / never* to talk about experiences in your life.
- My mum's **never used** the internet.
- **Have** you **ever blogged**?

Use the present perfect + *just* to talk about recent experiences.
- We've **just downloaded** Coldplay's new song.

We form the present perfect like this:
subject + *have* + past participle
The past participle is usually verb +*ed*. Some verbs have irregular past participles.

We use the present perfect for actions at an indefinite time and past simple for actions at a definite time in the past.	With the past simple we often use definite time expressions such as *yesterday, last year, three weeks ago.*
• They've **started** a computer course.	• They **started** a computer course last week.
• She's **just bought** a computer.	• She **bought** a computer yesterday.

A Complete the blog entry with the correct form of the present perfect.

Mike's blog   *March 20th*

Do you remember I told you about a girl I (1 *be*) ...... out with two or three times? I (2 *read*) ...... just ...... her blog. A friend gave me the address. In her blog she says she (3 *be*) ...... out with a really nice man a few times (– that's me!) But then she writes "I (4 *want*) ...... never ...... a long relationship. I (5 *have*) .... a good time but now it's finished – I (6 *send*) ...... just ...... him an email. Now I'm looking for a new boyfriend!" So I (7 *check*) ...... just ...... my email and it's true. She (8 *dump*) .... me!

B Write about:

1 Two things that you've done on a computer.
   a) ....
   b) ....
2 Two things you've never done in your life.
   a) ....
   b) ....
3 Two things that you've just done.
   a) ....
   b) ....

C Circle the correct form of the verb.

1 *Have you ever written / Did you ever write* anything for the internet?
2 I *'ve read / read* a really interesting news blog yesterday.
3 He *'s sent / sent* me an email five minutes ago.
4 My dad *has just started / just started* to write a book.
5 We *'ve never had / never had* any problems with our new internet company.
6 Last week I *'ve had / had* a terrible argument with my boyfriend in public.

Unit 7
For your eyes only — Workbook

2 Vocabulary

A How do you think these people are feeling? Match the adjectives to the people.

a) relieved	b) excited	c) proud
d) lonely	e) scared	f) upset

1 Gemma	"My parents have gone away on holiday. I really miss them." ………
2 Leo	"My exams are over at last." ………
3 Thomas	"I have a ticket for the *Black Eyed Peas* concert tomorrow. I can't wait!" ………
4 Mathilda	"My grandma has just died." ………
5 Louisa	"I've just won a website design competition." ………
6 Mark	"I hate flying. I'm not looking forward to my trip tomorrow." ………

B Complete the text with the correct words.

a) access	b) blogs	c) bloggers
d) brainstorm	e) editors	f) improve
g) post	h) spot	

Most (1) …… write about their personal experiences. But in America, college students are using (2) ……. in their classes. Anyone in the class with internet (3) …… can (4) …… ideas on a particular topic and (5) …… them on the class website. Professors say students have become more interested in their lessons. Some colleges are also using 'wikis': web pages where students are the (6) …… . Students can change things when they (7) …… mistakes. They can also (8) …… the pages by adding new ideas.

3 Pronunciation: Strong and weak forms

A lot of English words have *strong* and *weak* forms. Usually we use the *weak* forms.

A Listen and repeat these sentences.
1 Writers post details about their lives **and** thoughts.
2 Sam has just proposed **to** me.
3 I write without **an** editor changing things.
4 Here are some tips **for** writers.

We use the *strong* form when the word comes at the end of a sentence or when the word is emphasised.

B Listen and repeat these sentences.
1 This blog isn't just about me – it's about me **and** you.
2 I had nobody to talk **to**.
3 He hasn't just got **an** editor, he's got three!
4 What did you do that **for**?

Look at these sentences. Are the words in bold *strong* [S] or *weak* [W] forms? Mark them.

C Listen and check your answers.
1 I wrote about it in my blog, **of** course. ☐
2 Where does Salam Pax come **from**? ☐
3 She's **at** her desk. ☐
4 I'm not **as** clever as you – I'm cleverer! ☐

4 Use of English

A Complete the second sentence so that it means the same as the first.

1 I finished my piece of writing a minute ago.
   I've …… my piece of writing.
2 The first sentence really gets your attention.
   The first sentence is a real …… .
3 She writes full-time.
   She's a full-time …… .
4 It's an interesting blog, that's why I like it.
   I like the blog …… it's interesting.
5 My life isn't a public thing.
   My life is a …… thing.

5 Portfolio Writing

A Write an email to a friend and tell him/her about something exciting (real or imaginary) that you have just done (70–80 words).

B Write an essay with the title 'What do you keep private?' Explain what you do in public and what you prefer to do in private and why (120–150 words).

C Write a description of how the internet has changed since people first started using it. Think about how many people use it, who uses it, and what people use it for (120–150 words).

17

Unit 8 Fashionistas — Workbook

See pages 36–39

1 Language: articles

Use the indefinite article *a / an*:
- to talk about something for the first time
- to talk about something which isn't special or particular
- with jobs
- to mean *every*

- Paolo is **a** fashion model.
- **A** car arrived
- **An** ordinary day
- He's **a** teacher
- She's **a** doctor
- Twice **a** week
- £250 **a** month
- Sixty kilometres **an** hour

Use the definite article *the*:
- to talk about something again
- to talk about something in particular
- to talk about something unique (there is only one)
- with superlative adjectives
- with some proper nouns, for example seas, rivers and mountains

- when **the** car arrived
- **the** car was a Peugeot
- **the** sun
- **the** Queen
- **the** best
- **the** worst
- **the** Mediterranean
- **the** Thames
- **the** Alps

Use no article:
- to talk about something in general
- with most proper nouns, for example names of people, streets
- with the names of most countries
- BUT not for certain countries
- in some phrases

- He hates fashion.
- We met George.
- We walked to Oxford Street.
- I was in Italy.
- **the** UK • **the** USA • **the** Netherlands
- at home / at work / at college
- go to work / to school / to university
- in hospital / in bed / in prison

A Circle the correct article.

1 Paris, *a / the* beautiful capital on *the / –* Seine in *the / –* France, has always been *the / a* world's centre of haute couture fashion.
2 *The / –* fashion for *the / –* dogs is a new trend in *the / –* USA. *A / The* fashion hasn't reached *the / –* Britain yet.
3 *The / –* Kate Moss is *a / the* fashion model. When she is at *the / –* work she earns about $10,000 *a / the* day.
4 London Fashion Week takes place twice *a / the* year in *the / –* UK's capital. You can see *the / –* latest clothes from *the / –* most important British designers.
5 *The / –* people are starting to name their children after *the / –* brands. *The / –* most popular names from *a / the* world of fashion are Armani for *the / –* girls and Timberland for *the / –* boys.

B Complete the text with *a*, *the* or no article (✖).

Vivienne Westwood is (1) … successful designer: she sells clothes worth £50 million (2) … year. She never follows (3) … trends. (4) … clothes she designs always have (5) … individual style. She started designing (6) … clothes with Malcolm McLaren, manager of (7) … famous punk band, (8) … Sex Pistols. They had (9) … fashion shop in (10) … Chelsea, London; (11) … shop's name was 'Sex'. Vivienne Westwood has always been (12) … controversial person. She went to meet (13) … Queen at (14) … Buckingham Palace without wearing (15) … underwear.

Unit 8
Fashionistas Workbook

2 Vocabulary

A Find two more words for each list.

Footwear	Outerwear
• shoes	• jacket

Sportswear	Underwear
• shorts	• socks

B Complete the sentences with the correct words.

1 I don't like tight clothes; I prefer my clothes to be …… .
2 He never wears …… shirts. They're always patterned or checked or striped.
3 She wears a lot of ……: expensive earrings and necklaces.
4 My sister likes people to notice her. She always wears bright, …… clothes.
5 Pop stars often wear …… to hide their face.

C Describe what you are wearing today.

……………………………………………………
……………………………………………………
……………………………………………………

D Complete the poster with the correct words from the box.

a) exploit	b) globalisation	c) organic
d) factories	e) suppliers	f) sustainable

To all fashion fans

Stop (1) ……… ! Don't buy clothes from big global companies with (2) ……… in poor countries. These often (3) ……… the workers in their (4) ……… and pollute our environment. Support (5) ……… cotton farmers and buy (6) ……… clothing!

3 Word building

A You can make negative adjectives by adding negative prefixes. Find the negatives of the words in the box and put them in the table.

comfortable	expensive	fashionable
formal	organised	polite	possible	satisfied

dis-	in-	im-	un-
dishonest	**in**definite	**im**perfect	**un**cool

4 Use of English

A Complete the second sentence, so that it means the same as the first.

1 I haven't been to a fashion show.
   I've …… been to a fashion show.
2 I like buying shoes more than buying clothes.
   I …… buying shoes to buying clothes.
3 He wasn't happy with his new trainers.
   He was …… with his new trainers.
4 I left my sunglasses in the café.
   I …… take my sunglasses with me.
5 I'm not interested in fashion.
   I don't …… about fashion.

5 Portfolio Writing

A Your penfriend sends you a letter and tells you about her new mobile phone. Write a reply and tell her about your phone and how you use it. Or say why you like or dislike mobile phones in general (70–80 words).

B Write a description of some of your favourite clothes and accessories (120–150 words).

C Describe your idea of the life of a famous fashion designer or model (120–150 words).

19

Units 1–8 Progress check 1 — Workbook (See pages 8–41)

1 Language

A Complete these sentences.

1 Did you…	a) eat for breakfast?
2 Have you ever…	b) upset you?
3 When did you…	c) go shopping at the weekend?
4 Has your best friend ever…	d) last use a computer?
5 What did you…	e) made a fashion mistake?
6 What have you…	f) just done?

B Answer the questions in A about you. Give extra information.

1 Did you go shopping at the weekend?
　……………………………………………………
2 ……………………………………………………
3 ……………………………………………………
4 ……………………………………………………
5 ……………………………………………………
6 ……………………………………………………

C Complete the magazine article. Use the correct form of the present perfect, the past simple or *going to*.

In 1999 tennis stars Venus and Serena Williams (1 *win*) …… the French Open doubles and (2 *become*) …… the first sisters to win an important tennis title together. As doubles partners they (3 *win*) ……… all the major championships and both sisters (4 *achieve*) …… the World Number 1 ranking as singles players. They (5 *compete*) …… against each other many times. In 2001, for example, Venus (6 *defeat*) …… her sister in the final of the US Open. In 2002, Serena (7 *beat*) …… Venus in the Wimbledon final – and then a year later she (8 *do*) …… it again! What (9 *do*) …… the sisters …… next? Well, Serena would perhaps like to be an actress. Venus is already at design college and (10 *be*) …… a fashion designer. Good luck, girls!

D Choose an adjective and compare these things. Then write two more comparisons about music.

1 Hip hop is ………… than pop.
2 Alicia Keys is ………… singer around at the moment.
3 The Rio Carnival is ……… the Notting Hill Carnival.
4 The Live 8 concert was ………… concert I've ever seen.
5 DJ mixing is ……………. than writing songs.
6 ………………………………………………………
7 ………………………………………………………

E Complete Anna's email with *an*, *the* or no article (✘).

Hi Jess!
It's my first day on (1) …… holiday. It's much better than being at (2) ……. college! (3) …… day didn't start too well, though. I booked (4) …… taxi to (5) …… station, but (6) …… car was late. I nearly missed (7) …… train! Anyway, I left (8) …… London about 6 o'clock in the morning and went through (9) …… Channel Tunnel. I didn't enjoy being underground but we were in (10) …… France very quickly. The Eurostar train travels really fast – 260km (11) …… hour! I changed trains in (12) ….. Paris and travelled down to (13) …… Mediterranean to meet my friend Lucy. She's just finished working as (14) …… au pair in Nice. We're going to have (15) ……… great time on our holiday!
Love Anna

F Circle the correct answer.

1 I …….. go to football matches. I've only seen one match this year.
　a) always　b) sometimes　c) hardly ever
2 I don't like chips ………. . They taste disgusting and they make you fat.
　a) at all　b) much　c) a little
3 I decided to go to college in Manchester ….. I've got a lot of friends there.
　a) and　b) because　c) but
4 I watched my favourite programme, then I watched two DVDs and listened to some music. ……… I went to bed.
　a) First　b) Next　c) Finally
5 I like his style, he dresses really ………… .
　a) badly　b) good　c) well

Progress check 1 Workbook

Units 1–8

2 Vocabulary

A Put the words in the correct lists. Then add another word to each list.

a) accountant	b) bruise
c) computer programmer	d) cut
e) documentary	f) reporter
g) dairy produce	h) fruit
i) soap opera	j) series
k) sprained knee	l) editor
m) vegetables	n) viewers
o) swollen ankle	p) meat

Food	Jobs
Sports injuries	**TV programmes**

B Circle the correct adjective.
1 Mmm, this cake is *delicious / patterned*.
2 BMX biking is a *lonely / dangerous* sport.
3 I usually wear *baggy / challenging* clothes.
4 He's got very *controversial / tasty* opinions.
5 I prefer *pushy / plain* T-shirts.

C Complete the dialogue.

a) cash	b) customer	c) jackets	d) pay
e) receipt	f) refund	g) sale	h) shirt
i) store card	j) wallet		

Assistant Next (1) …… please. Hello.
Dan Hello, I'd like to return this (2) …… . It's too small.
Assistant Have you got your (3) ……?
Dan Yes, I have.
Assistant Hmm, it was in the (4) …… , so I can't give you a (5) ……Would you like anything else?
Dan You've got some black (6) …… over there. How much are they?
Assistant Er, they're £40.
Dan OK. I'll take one of those.
Assistant Right, that's £20. Have you got a (7) ………?
Dan No, I haven't. And I don't want one.
Assistant Oh, OK. How would you like to (8)………, then?
Dan By (9) ……., please. Oh, no. Where's my (10) …..? It's gone!

D Complete the mind maps. Add as many words as you can. Add new circles if you need to.

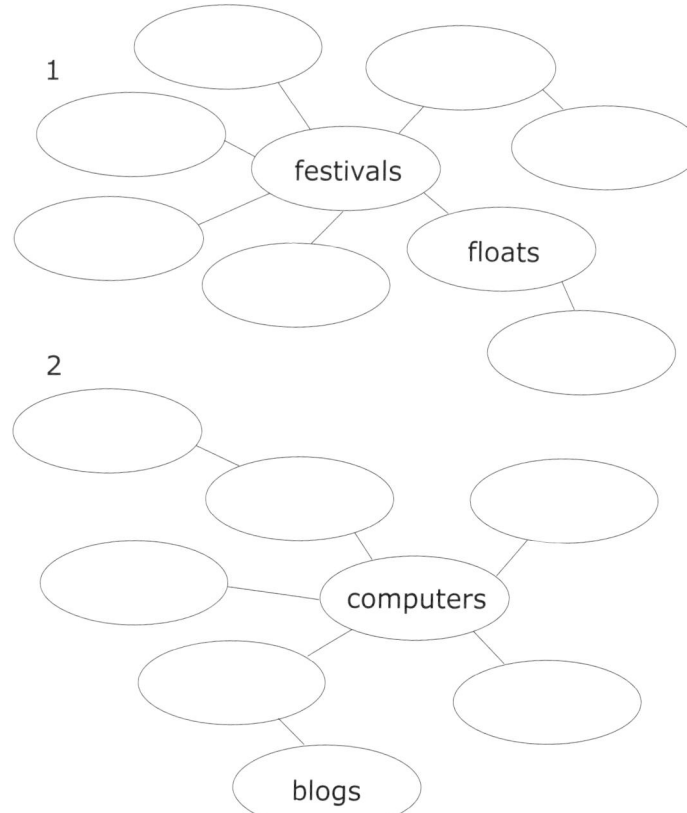

E On what part of your body do you wear these things?
1 hat ……………………………
2 scarf ……………………………
3 sunglasses ……………………………
4 trainers ……………………………
5 necklace ……………………………
6 watch ……………………………
7 sandals ……………………………
8 make-up ……………………………

F Write definitions for these words.
1 A blog is ……………………………………
2 Global warming is …………………………..
3 Skydiving is …………………………………
4 Jewellery is …………………………………
5 Online shopping is …………………………
6 Sponsorship is ………………………………
7 A chairperson is ……………………………
8 Globalisation is ……………………………

Unit 9 Rule of law — Workbook

See pages 42–45

1 Language: Obligation and necessity: *must, have to* and *need*

To express obligation or necessity, use *must, have to* and *need to*.	To express lack of obligation or necessity, use *don't have to* or *don't need to*.
• You **must** put your litter in the bin. • You **have to** be quiet in the library. • I **need to** go to the toilet.	• You **don't have to** wear smart clothes, but it's a good idea. • I **don't need to** have a shower.

Must doesn't have its own past tense form.
The past tense of both *have to* and *must* is *had to*.

• We **had to** revise for an English test last week.

A Complete the text with the correct form of *(not) have to* and the verb.

Many countries have banned the free use of plastic bags. In Ireland shops (1) *(to pay)* …… a tax for each bag they provide. Shops (2) *(to pass)* …… this tax on to their customers. Shoppers (3) *(to pay)* …… 15 cents for each bag and the charge for the bag (4) *(to be)* …… on the receipt. Some small plastic bags are still free: customers (5) *(to buy)* …… bags for meat and fish. And the shop still (6) …… *(to charge)* for bags for unpacked foods like vegetables or sweets.

B Circle the correct form of the verb.
1 We *have to / don't have to* hurry. We have lots of time.
2 She *had to / have to* leave the cinema because her mobile phone rang.
3 I'm cold. I *need to / don't need to* drink a hot cup of coffee.
4 Smoking isn't allowed here. You *must / don't have to* put out your cigarette.
5 She *didn't need to / had to* go to the bank because she had enough money.

2 Connections

Do these words and expressions go with *do* or *make*? Put them in the correct lists.

a decision	an English course	your homework	a phone call	what you want
a mistake	laws	a test	the shopping	dinner

do	make
1 • an English course	6 • a decision
2	7
3	8
4	9
5	10

Unit 9

Rule of law Workbook

3 Vocabulary

A Complete the sentences with the correct words.

| a) fraud | b) graffiti | c) dropping litter |
| d) murder | e) smoking | |

1 A lot of people think ...... isn't a crime; it's an art form.
2 Credit card ...... is increasing.
3 ...... makes the streets look untidy and can cause pollution.
4 ...... is bad for your health – and bad for other people's health, too.
5 I read a terrible story in the paper about the ...... of a child. He was only three years old when he died.

B Complete the sentences with the correct verbs. Then put the sentences in the correct order.

a) ...... The manager of the shop ...... the police.
b) ..*1*.. My cousin Vinny ...... the law regularly.
c) ...... The police came and ...... him.
d) ...... Vinny ...... in prison again now.
e) ...... Last week Vinny ...... another crime – he stole some stuff from a clothes shop.

4 Pronunciation: Stress on auxiliary verbs

(14) English stresses the most important words in a sentence.

A Listen and mark the stressed verbs.
1 I can phone her on my mobile.
2 Do you smoke?
3 You must remember to wash your hands.
4 Those people are breaking the law.
5 Excuse me, I need to get out here.

B Circle the correct alternative to complete the rule.
• We usually / don't usually stress auxiliary verbs.

(14) Sometimes we stress auxiliary verbs to emphasise them, or to express strong feelings.

C Listen and repeat the sentences.
1 Oh no! Look at the room. What have you done?
2 We don't have a choice; we must call the police.
3 I can't do it!
4 You can do it if you really try.
5 Please, I need to speak to him now!
6 Let's stay a bit longer; we don't have to leave now.

5 Use of English

A Complete the second sentence so that it means the same as the first.

1 You can go into the museum without a ticket.	You ...... a ticket for the museum.
2 It isn't honest to copy your friend's homework.	It's ...... to copy your friend's homework.
3 Smoking in restaurants is illegal here.	Smoking in restaurants is against ...... here.
4 It isn't necessary to shout.	You ...... shout.
5 You shouldn't break laws.	You should ...... laws.

6 Portfolio Writing

A Write an article explaining why you would like or wouldn't like to live in a commune (120–150 words).

B You have just visited a place (perhaps a cinema or restaurant) which had rules you didn't agree with. Write a letter or an email to the place and give your opinion and reasons (70–80 words).

C Write an essay with the title 'Do we need rules?' Think about the protection of people and the environment and about personal freedom (120–150 words).

23

Unit 10 What's next? Workbook

See pages 46–49

1 Language: *will* future for predictions

We use the *will* future to make general predictions about the future.
• Everyone **will** have a robot by 2050.   • I'll live in a different country when I'm older.
The negative of *will* is *will not*, or *won't*.
• We **won't** have robots by 2050.   • I **won't** live in a different country.
The interrogative of *will* is *will you* / *will she* / *will they*?
• **Will they** have robots by 2050?   • **Will you** live in a different country?
We often use these phrases with the *will* future:
• **I think** we'll live in very different houses.   • I'll **probably** have a scientific job.
• **I'm sure that** the future **will** be great.   • I'll **definitely** have a lot of children.
We use *will* for predictions … and …   ***going to* for plans and intentions.**
• **What will** happen in the future?   • **I'm going to** watch a DVD tonight.

A Write Oliver's predictions about his life in five years.

| • be a teacher ✓ | • live in London ✓ | • travel a lot ✓ |
| • be rich ✗ | • have my own flat ✗ | • be married ✗ |

In five years, I ....
....

B Complete the text with the correct form of the *will* future.

What (1 *happen*) …… in the future? Nobody knows. But in the year 2000, a lot of surveys predicted life in the twenty-first century. According to one survey, people are pessimistic about technology. Most people think we (2 *take*) …… holidays in space and that we (3 *discover*) …… other life in space. Only 15% of people think that these things (4 *probably / happen*) …… . What social changes (5 *take place*) …… ? Most people are optimistic. A third of people are sure that living standards (6 *get*) …… better. Most people think there (7 *be*) …… another world war. But unfortunately a lot of people think that there (8 *be*) …… small wars in lots of different countries.

C Write three predictions about the future. Use *will* or *won't*.
1 ....
2 ....
3 ....

D Complete the sentences with *will* or *going to*.
1 I got some money for my birthday, so I (*buy*) ….. a new mobile phone.
2 (*you / see*) …. the new science fiction film? It's really good.
3 Computer technology (*develop*) …… very quickly in the next ten years.
4 New developments in cars (*not change*) ….. the pollution problems.
5 We (*do*) ….. our technology project on the history of inventions.

Unit 10
What's next? Workbook

2 Vocabulary

A Match the descriptions with the correct inventions in the box.

a) telephone	b) wheels
c) digital camera	d) washing machine
e) DVD player	f) flat screen TV

1 You can watch your favourite programmes on this and it doesn't take up too much space. ......
2 It makes your clothes clean. ......
3 You can take pictures with this and then keep the pictures on your computer or print them out. ......
4 Your bike or car can't move without them. ......
5 This plays music and also films in different languages. ......
6 You use it to talk to your friends. ......

B Complete the instructions for a new computer. Choose the correct words:

1 Find an electrical   a) plug   b) socket
2 Plug in the computer using the white   a) button   b) cable
3 Connect the printer using the USB   a) port   b) switch
4 Insert the software CD into the   a) program   b) drive
5 Follow the instructions on the   a) appliance   b) screen

C Complete the sentences with the words from the box.

a) test	b) experiments	c) solve
d) laboratory	e) robots	

1 I work in a scientific ....
2 Our scientists do ...... to discover new things.
3 Sometimes there are problems we cannot ....
4 We use ...... to help us make very small products.
5 We ...... all our products.

D Match the time words with the correct definitions.

1	day	a)	sixty seconds
2	century	b)	three hundred and sixty-five days
3	decade	c)	ten years
4	minute	d)	twenty-four hours
5	year	e)	a hundred years

3 Word Building

A Complete the tables.

Verb	Noun	Noun	Adjective
invent	1	science	6
2	development	7	technological
inform	3	optimism	8
4	solution	9	magical
communicate	5	ignorance	10

4 Use of English

A Complete the second sentence so that it means the same as the first.

1 In my opinion, intelligent robots will never exist.
   I ...... intelligent robots will ever exist.
2 Futurists predict the future.
   Futurists make ...... about the future.
3 I'm certain that everybody will have wireless technology soon.
   Everybody will ...... have wireless technology soon.
4 Alexander Bell invented the telephone in 1876.
   Alexander Bell invented the telephone ...... ago.

5 Portfolio Writing

A Write an email or letter to a friend and tell him or her about a new appliance or gadget you have bought (70–80 words).

B Write an essay about the future. What are you optimistic about? What are you pessimistic about? (120–150 words).

25

Unit 11 Travel costs — Workbook

See pages 50–53

1 Language: present perfect with *for* and *since*

You know we can use present perfect to talk about the recent and indefinite past.
- I've **been** to the USA.
- I've just **visited** China.

We use the present perfect with *for* and *since* to talk about the duration of events which are still continuing.

Use *for* with a period of time. 	Use *since* with a starting point in time. 
• I've been at college **for** one year. • He's been my boyfriend **for** two months.	• I've lived here **since** 2003. • I've known my best friend **since** we were small.

We also use the present perfect for events that started in the past and connect to the future.

A Complete the sentences with *for* or *since*.
1. We've had our car ...... five years.
2. I've known him ...... 2002.
3. I haven't used the bus ...... I got a new bike.
4. The Channel Tunnel has been open ...... 1994.
5. We haven't travelled by train ...... years.
6. The airport has been closed ...... three hours.

B Write sentences with the present perfect and *for* or *since*.
1. I / like / horseriding / a long time.
2. Cheap airlines / be / popular / the 1980s.
3. We / use / the Channel Tunnel / it opened.
4. My boyfriend and I / have / a motorbike / two years.
5. I / fly / three times / the beginning of the year.

Time expressions with the present perfect and past simple

Use the present perfect for actions at an indefinite time in the past or for a period of time continuing to the present, with these expressions:	Use the past simple for a completely finished period of time, with these expressions:
• ever, never • just • for, since	• yesterday on Thursday / in 2000 / in May • last week, last month, last year • 3 years ago / two weeks ago

C Complete the text with the present perfect or the past simple.

Global warming (1 *be*) ...... a problem for years. Environmentalists (2 *start*) ...... to worry about it decades ago. But climate change (3 *only / become*) .... a big talking point since 1997. In 1997, the Kyoto climate conference (4 *take place*) ...... in Kyoto, Japan. At the conference many countries (5 *decide*) ...... to reduce the carbon dioxide they produce. The Kyoto Protocol officially (6 *become*) ...... law in February 2005. Countries such as Russia, China, Japan and Canada and most European countries (7 *just / start*) ...... to reduce their carbon dioxide. However, the USA and Australia (8 *not agree*) ...... to the Protocol.

2 Vocabulary

A Complete the travel brochure. Circle ⃝ the correct words.

Egypt is the perfect place for a (1) *relaxing / stressful* holiday. On our tour, you'll see Egypt using different types of (2) *traffic / transport*. On Day 1 we will see the sights of Cairo (3) *on / by* foot. In the evening we'll travel (4) *by / in* train to Ashwan where we'll spend Day 2. On Day 3 you can ride (5) *on / by* a camel in the desert – an exciting and very (6) *polluting / eco-friendly* method of transport! On Day 4 and Day 5 we'll sail down the River Nile on a luxury (7) *bus / boat*.
Remember we can arrange travel to Egypt. Most (8) *airlines / passengers* can fly you to Cairo and (9) *flights / planes* from Europe and the USA are fairly cheap – for example, you can fly from London for about £200 including (10) *tax / fare*.

B Complete the sentences about photosynthesis with the correct words.

a) cells	b) glucose	c) leaves
d) oxygen	e) respiration	f) roots
g) sunlight		

1 Plants take in water through their …… .
2 They take in carbon dioxide through their …… .
3 Photosynthesis takes place in leaf …… .
4 …… helps photosynthesis take place.
5 Photosynthesis produces …… and …… .
6 …… is the opposite process of photosynthesis.

3 Use of English

Complete the second sentence so that it means the same as the first.

1 When did you get your scooter?
   How long …… your scooter?
2 I'm sorry, that isn't very convenient.
   I'm sorry, that's very …… .
3 I've driven my own car since 2004.
   I got my own car …… ago.
4 We haven't got enough money to go on holiday.
   We can't …… to go on holiday.
5 Planes cause air pollution.
   Planes …… the air.

4 Pronunciation: Consonant clusters 1

🔊 Two or three consonants at the beginning of words can sometimes cause problems.

A Listen to these words and repeat.
1 **st**op, **st**udent, **str**ess
2 **sp**eak, **sp**ecial, **spr**ead
3 **sl**ow, **sl**im, **sl**eep
4 **sm**all, **sm**ile, **sm**oke
5 **Sc**otland, **sc**ary, **scr**eam

B 🔊 Listen and complete the words with the correct consonants.
1 …art   5 …een
2 …eet   6 …ell
3 …end   7 …ing
4 …edge   8 …ar

C 🔊 Listen and repeat these sentences.
1 Smart students from Scotland stop smoking.
2 Special stars smile on screen.

5 Portfolio Writing

A Write a letter or an email to a friend and tell him/her about a recent journey or holiday (70–80 words).
B Write an article for your college magazine about the importance of trees for our environment (120–150 words).
C Describe the traffic situation in your country. What methods of transport are popular? What are advantages / disadvantages? (120–150 words).

Unit 12 — Money, money, money — Workbook — See pages 54–57

1 Language: Modals of certainty and uncertainty: *will* and *might*

To express certainty about future activities, use *will*.	• In the future, more people will invest money. • I'll get a job in a bank.
To express uncertainty about future activities, use *might*.	• I might buy a lottery ticket. • It might be my lucky day.
Remember: • after modal verbs, use the infinitive without *to*. • don't use 'do' with *might* and *will* ...	
... to form negatives	• We won't (will not) borrow money. • I might not (mightn't) go out.
... to form questions	• Will they go to prison for stealing? • Might you go out tonight?

A Complete the sentences with *will / won't* or *might / might not*.

1 You ... get any money from the cashpoint. It's out of order.
2 I ... start using internet banking, but I'm not sure it's safe.
3 They ... believe you. But perhaps they will.
4 My parents always help me. They ... definitely lend me some money.
5 He ... get rich. He's too lazy.
6 The bank ... give us a credit card. They don't give them to everybody.
7 I'm sure you ... be successful because you're so good at maths.
8 We ... be lucky. Let's wait and see.

B Imagine you have won £100,000. Write two sentences about what you will definitely do with the money and two sentences about what you might do.

Too and *enough*

Use *too* before adjectives or quantifiers.	• He's **too** rich. • He's got **too much** money.
Use *enough* after adjectives, before nouns, or on its own.	• He isn't rich **enough**. • She hasn't got **enough** money. • Have you got **enough**?

C Thomas is very bad with money. Complete the sentences about him using the words in the box and *too* and *enough*.

| a) generous | b) good | c) many | d) money |

1 He isn't ...... at maths.
2 He's ...... to his friends.
3 He doesn't save ....
4 He buys ...... DVDs.

Unit 12

Money, money, money — Workbook

2 Vocabulary

A Complete the money crossword.

Across

3 how much money you can get for another country's money (8,4)
4 the money in your account (4, 7)
6 the money that a country uses (8)
8 get money and give it back later (6)
10 take illegally (5)
11 ask strangers for money (3)

Down

1 an arrangement with a bank to pay in and take out money (4,7)
2 get money by working (4)
5 you can get money here when the bank is closed (9)
6 metal money (5)
7 paper money (4)
9 keep money (4)

3 Connections

A Complete the phrases with the correct prepositions.
1 borrow money …… a friend
2 spend money …… clothes
3 invest money …… shares
4 save money …… the future
5 change money …… euros

B Find the opposites.
1 honest   →   ……
2 ……   ←   borrow
3 rich   →   ……
4 weak   →   ……

4 Use of English

A Complete the second sentence so that it means the same as the first.
1 The company needs people to invest.
   The company is looking for …… .
2 It's possible that the bank will close down.
   The bank …… close down.
3 The assistant didn't give me £10 change – she gave me £20.
   The assistant gave me £20 change …… £10.
4 The bank's opening hours are too short.
   The bank's opening hours aren't …… .
5 The customers were amazed.
   The customers were very …… .

5 Portfolio Writing

A You know a friend cheated in an exam and you aren't sure what to do. Write an email to another friend. Tell him/her what you think you might do and ask for advice (70–80 words).

B Write an article with the title 'Is money the most important thing in life?' Say why it is necessary in life, and why it is or isn't so important, or what things mean more to you (health, family, friends) (120–150 words).

C Write about a good or bad experience you had with money. Explain what happened and how you felt (120–150 words).

Unit 13 Destination disaster — Workbook (See pages 58–61)

1 Language: infinitive of purpose

> Use the infinitive with *to* to express the purpose of somebody's actions, or the purpose of a thing.
>
> - I use my bike **to go** to college.
> - He only has an expensive car **to impress** people.
>
> We also use *in order to* + infinitive to express purpose.
>
> - I wrote to my local newspaper **in order to** express my views about cars.

A Rewrite the sentences with an infinitive of purpose.

Example: She has a part-time job. She is saving for a new bike.
- She has a part-time job (in order) to save for a new bike.

1. The government is planning new laws. They want to stop aggressive driving.
2. I need my bike. I cycle to the station on it.
3. I'm going to take my driving test. I'd like to be more independent.
4. They are building more cycle lanes. They want to encourage more cyclists.
5. I wear a cycle helmet. It protects me against dangerous drivers.
6. I cycled to the newsagents. I bought a magazine.

B Complete the sentences about you with an infinitive of purpose.

1. I'd like to have a car ....
2. I'm learning English ....
3. I intend to study hard ....
4. I phone my friends ....
5. I use the internet ....

Order of adjectives

> Use adjectives in this order: *opinion + size + age + colour*
>
> - My uncle has bought a **fantastic new** car. (**opinion + age**)
> - My bike has a **big brown** basket on the front. (**size + colour**)

C Put the sentences in the correct order.

1. old / my / Fiat / drives / tiny / mum / a
2. new / motorway / a / planning / they're / big
3. like / Ferrari / cool / a / red / I'd
4. accidents / young / often / inexperienced / cause / drivers
5. has / an / black / bike / saddle / uncomfortable / my

D Describe:

1. The bag or backpack you take to lessons. ....
2. The car you'd like to have. ....

Destination disaster Workbook

2 Vocabulary

A Match the words with the correct definitions.

1	A car has four and a bike has two of these.	a) pedals
2	It controls the direction of a car.	b) exhaust pipe
3	You control the direction of a bike with these.	c) wheels
4	You sit on this on a bike.	d) handlebars
5	This is where engine gases come out.	e) steering wheel
6	You move these things on a bike with your feet.	f) helmet
7	You wear this on your head.	g) saddle

B Complete the newspaper report with the correct words.

a) accident	b) braked	c) crashed
d) junction	e) traffic lights	f) vehicles
g) traffic jams	h) overtook	

Yesterday there was a terrible (1) ..... on Bristol Road. It involved six (2) .... It happened when a car (3) ..... another car just before a (4) ...... The driver didn't realise the (5) ..... were red and had to move back in front of the other car. The car behind (6) ..... but couldn't slow down enough. It (7) ..... into the car in front and others did the same. There were long (8) ..... for an hour after the accident.

3 Pronunciation: Consonant clusters 2

Two or three consonants at the end of words can sometimes cause problems.

A Listen to these words and repeat them.
1 fa**st**, cycli**st**
2 accide**nt**, importa**nt**
3 behi**nd**, girlfrie**nd**
4 thi**nk**, ta**nk**
5 a**sk**, de**sk**

B Listen and complete the words with the correct consonants.
1 pa...   5 ba...
2 spe...   6 inte...
3 di...   7 te...
4 fro...   8 sou...

C Listen and repeat these sentences.
1 Fast cyclists have accidents.
2 My girlfriend intends to take her test.

4 Use of English

Complete the second sentence so that it means the same as the first.

1 It's possible I won't pass my driving test.
   I .... not pass my driving test.
2 I have a new helmet which is blue.
   I have a .... helmet.
3 They drove as fast as they could.
   They drove at full ....
4 A lot of teenagers think that.
   That's the .... of a lot of teenagers.
5 You drive well.
   You're a ....
6 The driver drove more quickly.
   The driver ....

5 Portfolio Writing

A Write a letter or an email to a friend and tell him/her about a car or bicycle you intend to buy. What is it like? Why do you need it or when do you intend to use it? (70–80 words).

B You have formed an anti-car or pro-car group at your college. Write an article for your college magazine explaining what your group intends to do and why (120–150 words).

C Imagine you saw an accident or a road rage incident recently. Describe what happened (120–150 words).

Unit 14 All in the family — Workbook

See pages 62–65

1 Language: past continuous

Use the past continuous for actions in progress in the past.
- At eight o'clock I **was lying** in bed.
- I **was reading** a book all yesterday afternoon.

Form the past continuous like this:
- Subject + *was / were* + verb + *-ing*

We often use the past continuous to describe the background to completed actions. For completed actions, use the past simple.
- Everybody **was waiting** in the church when Lucy **came** in.
- While we **were dancing**, Dad **fell** over.

A Complete the text with the correct form of the past continuous.

Yesterday afternoon I (1 *think*) …… about my graduation day. It was one of the best days of my life! It (2 *rain*) …… when we got to the college but I felt really happy. I was one of the last people on stage. I (3 *start*) …… to get very nervous when they called my name. I got my certificate and waved to my family. My dad and my sister (4 *smile*) …… at me …… and they (5 *clap*) …… My mum (6 *cry*) …… of course, but she (7 *clap*) …… , too. At home my grandparents and aunt and uncles (8 *wait*) …… for us and we had a great family party.

B Circle the correct verb.
1. I *got / was getting* ready for the party when my friend *phoned / was phoning*.
2. What *did you do / were you doing* all day yesterday?
3. Mum *made / was making* dinner quickly while we *watched / were watching* TV.
4. They *got / were getting* engaged and then *got / were getting* married a month later.
5. The sun *shone / was shining* when we woke up.
6. We *had / were having* a great time at my sister's wedding. I'll always remember it.

C Complete the sentences about you.
1. At six o'clock this morning I ……
2. At ten o'clock this morning I ……
3. At twelve o'clock midday I ……

2 Use of English

Complete the second sentence so that it means the same as the first.
1. We saved up because we wanted to get married.
   We saved up …… get married.
2. Single parent families are very common in Britain.
   There are …… of single parent families in Britain.
3. Their son is grown up now.
   Their son is an …… now.
4. She does nothing in the house.
   She doesn't do …… in the house.
5. I fell asleep during my dad's speech.
   I fell asleep …… my dad was giving his speech.

Unit 14

All in the family Workbook

3 Vocabulary

A Find the words for special occasions.

thri**b**	• birth
vren**a**yairns	
hadryti**b**	
gid**w**end	
trio**g**adaun	

B Complete the text with the correct form of the words in the box.

a) bridesmaids	b) divorced	c) get engaged
d) get married	e) honeymoon	f) reception
g) wedding	h) witnesses	

In 1981, Prince Charles of England (1) ...... to Lady Diana Spencer. Six months later, their famous (2) ...... took place in St Paul's Cathedral in London. Three thousand five hundred people were at the church and about 750 million people were watching the event on TV. Diana wore a wonderful dress and had five (3) .... Later there was a (4) ...... for 120 family guests at Buckingham Palace before the couple left for their (5) ...... in the south of England and then the Mediterranean. Fifteen years later, they were (6) .... Diana died in a car accident in 1997. In 2005, Prince Charles (7) ...... to Camilla Parker Bowles in a very different wedding. Charles' and Camilla's sons were their (8) ....

C Complete the definitions.

1 A couple who have no children are ....
2 A child who has no brothers or sisters is an ....
3 The daughter of your father and his new wife is your ....
4 The children of your father's new wife are his ....
5 A man or woman who looks after children alone is a ....
6 A family where parents and children live with grandparents and other family members is an ....

4 Pronunciation: Intonation in statements

A 🎧 Listen to these statements from the listening activity 5 in Unit 14. Does the speaker's voice rise [↗] or fall [↘]?
1 The guests will be here soon. [......]
2 He was watching sport on TV. [......]
3 He hasn't cooked more than five meals in twenty-five years. [......]
4 I did the ironing last night. [......]

B 🎧 Now listen to these statements. Does the speaker's voice rise [↗] or fall [↘] ? Why?
1 The guests will be here in five minutes. [......]
2 He's on the phone. [......]
3 She's making pasta. [......]
4 You did the washing yesterday. [......]

C Complete the rules.
• When the speaker is certain the information is correct, his / her voice ......
• When the speaker is uncertain if the information is correct, his / her voice ......

D 🎧 Listen to these sentences. Is the speaker certain or uncertain?
1 She's sixteen years old. ......
2 He's very unhappy. ......
3 He's an only child. ......
4 The wedding's in two weeks. ......

5 Portfolio Writing

A Write an email to a new penfriend and tell him / her about your family. Ask questions about your penfriend's family (70–80 words).

B Write an answer to the question: 'Families: hell or happiness?' Describe the role of families in your society and say how important your family is to you (120–150 words).

C Describe a special occasion that you have been to. What was the occasion? What happened? Did you enjoy it? Why or why not? (120–150 words).

Unit 15 The new epidemics — Workbook — See pages 66–69

1 Language: zero and first conditional

Use the zero conditional to talk about general facts.
- If people eat too much, they become overweight.
- If you smoke, you can get cancer.

We form the zero conditional like this:
If + present simple: present simple or modal verb

Use the first conditional to talk about events that will probably happen in the future.
- If we go swimming twice a week, we'll get fit.
- If her headache gets worse, she won't come to the concert.

We form the first conditional like this:
If + present simple: *will* future or modal verb

Word order: the *if-clause* can be the first or second clause in the sentence.
When it is the first clause, use a comma after it.
- **If** you go to bed early, you'll feel better.

When it is the second clause, you don't need a comma.
- You'll feel better **if** you go to bed early.

unless* means *if not
- You won't get better **unless** you go to the doctor.
= You won't get better *if* you *don't* go to the doctor.

A Match the sentence halves.
1. If people eat too much unhealthy food,
2. If the weather is bad,
3. If you drink a small amount of red wine,
4. If people work too hard,
5. If hospitals aren't clean,
6. If people are happy,

a) infections spread.
b) they are healthy.
c) they can get heart disease.
d) I feel depressed.
e) it improves your health.
f) they get stressed.

B Emily is thinking about getting fit. Complete her sentences with the correct form of the verb.

If I do some exercise, I (1 *get*) .... fitter. I think I'll start jogging. But I (2 *need*) ...... new shoes and new sports clothes if I go jogging – that'll be expensive. And if I (3 *not be*) ...... careful, I might sprain my ankle or hurt my knees. When can I go? If I go in the morning, I (4 *have to get up*) ...... early and I (5 *not get*) ...... enough sleep. But I'll miss my favourite TV programmes if I (6 *go*) .... in the evening. Hmm. So if I (7 *not start*) ...... jogging, I'll save money, I (8 *not get*) .... sports injuries, I (9 *not feel*) ... tired and I (10 *not miss*) ...... the soaps. No jogging for me, then!

C Rewrite the sentences with *unless*.
1. If he doesn't stop drinking, he'll destroy his health. *Unless* ....
2. If we don't hurry, the chemist will be closed. *Unless* ....
3. If it doesn't rain, we'll play tennis. *Unless* ....
4. If the government doesn't invest in healthcare, the system will break down. *Unless* ....
5. If you don't take your medicine, you won't get better. *Unless* ....

Unit 15 — The new epidemics — Workbook

2 Vocabulary

A Complete the sentences with the correct words.

| a) an injection | b) antibiotics | c) an aspirin |
| d) tissues | e) medicine | |

1. Just take ...... and your headache will go.
2. That's a terrible cough! Do you want some cough ......?
3. If the infection gets worse, you should get some ...... from the doctor.
4. I always have ...... against hay fever in the spring.
5. Oh dear. I think I'm getting a cold and I don't have any ....

B Circle the correct alternatives.

People first recognised AIDS as a (1) *virus / disease* in 1982. Since then AIDS has become a global (2) *epidemic / allergy*. We all know that the HIV (3) *virus / disease* causes AIDS and that it is highly (4) *infection / infectious*. It is possible to prevent (5) *infectious / infection* and (6) *drugs / vaccines* can slow down the disease. But without a (7) *virus / vaccine* against HIV, AIDS will continue to (8) *spread / stop*.

C Complete the dialogue with the words in the box.

| a) passive smoking | b) genetic | c) exercise |
| d) heart disease | e) a balanced diet | |

Doctor: So you feel tired all the time?
Patient: Yes, that's right.
Doctor: Do you eat (1) ......?
Patient: Yes, I think so, lots of fruit and vegetables.
Doctor: What about (2) ......?
Patient: Er, I walk to the bus stop every morning.
Doctor: You need to do a bit more than that! Do you smoke?
Patient: Well, not too many.
Doctor: Hmm, you know you're not just harming yourself but other people as well through (3) .... Is there any (4) ... in your family?
Patient: Yes, actually. My father died of it. Is it (5) ......?
Doctor: It can be. Let's check a few things.

3 Connections

A Complete the phrases with the correct prepositions.

1. be ...... hospital
2. go ...... the doctor
3. die ...... a disease
4. protect yourself ...... infection
5. be ill ...... flu

4 Word building

A Complete the table with the correct nouns.

Verb	Noun
die	1
live	2
ache	3
prevent	4
protect	5

5 Use of English

A Complete the second sentence so that it means the same as the first.

1. I think our healthcare system is quite good.
   In my ......, our healthcare system is quite good.
2. More and more people are getting cancer.
   The number of people with cancer is ....
3. I won't go to the doctor's if you don't come with me.
   I won't go to the doctor ...... you come with me.
4. My advice is to enjoy life.
   You ...... enjoy life.
5. During the football match, I suddenly felt sick.
   While I ...... football, I suddenly felt sick.

6 Portfolio Writing

A A hypochondriac friend has sent you an email telling you she has terrible headaches. Write a reply (70–80 words).

B Write an essay on smoking. Think of the arguments for and against smoking and give your personal opinion (120–150 words).

Unit 16 Adventures in language — Workbook — See pages 70–73

1 Language: present continuous for future arrangements

> You know we use the present continuous for actions which are happening now.
> - He's meeting his friends now.
> - She's getting ready for the party at the moment.
>
> Use *going to* for future intentions.
> - I'm going to watch an English film.
>
> We can also use the present continuous for arrangements in the future.
> - We're doing a language course in the summer holidays.
>
> *Going to* is often possible instead of the present continuous. But when we talk about future arrangements, the present continuous is more usual.
> - He's meeting his friends later.
> - He's going to meet his friends later.

A Complete the dialogue with the correct form of the present continuous.

Dan   What are you doing this evening?
Tim   I (1 *help*) …… Xavier with his end of term essay. I (2 *go*) …. to his house and we (3 *check*) …… his English together. He's worried about his grammar. What about you? (4 *play*) …… you …… football this evening?
Dan   No, our team (5 *not play*) …… today. Baz (6 *come*) …… round on his new motorbike. He (7 *take*) ……. me for a ride on it and then we (8 *have*) …… a pizza at the café.
Tim   Well, that sounds more fun than checking English grammar!

B Victoria has a busy day tomorrow. Write sentences about her day.

9.30   Doctor's
11.00 Meet Emma in town
13.00 Lunch with Emma and Mel
16.00 Hairdresser's
20.00 Dinner with David

At 9.30 Victoria is ………………………………
At 11.00 she ………………………………
At 13.00 Victoria, Emma and Mel ………………………………
At 16.00 she ………………………………
At 20.00 Victoria and David ………………………………

C Write three sentences about your arrangements for next week.

………………………………………………………………………………………………………
………………………………………………………………………………………………………
………………………………………………………………………………………………………

D Write three sentences about your intentions for the next few days.

………………………………………………………………………………………………………
………………………………………………………………………………………………………
………………………………………………………………………………………………………

Unit 16

Adventures in language — Workbook

2 Vocabulary

A Who is doing what in the holidays? Match the holiday plans with the correct people.

| a) do a language course |
| b) go on a family holiday |
| c) stay at home |
| d) go to an activity camp |
| e) look after brothers and sisters |
| f) hang out with friends |

1 ... Tom   "We're not doing anything special; we're just going to meet at each other's houses and in town."
2 ... Becky "My parents are working so I'm the babysitter. We'll probably go to the park and the swimming pool a lot."
3 ... Ben   "I'm doing a windsurfing course and I'm going to try water skiing too." I'm looking forward to being away from home."
4 ... Lucy   "My friend and I are going to Oxford for two weeks. We want to get lots of English practice before the exams."
5 ... Amy   "We're going to Spain. We're going to lie on the beach all day and do nothing!"
6 ... Matt   "We're not going away. I'm going to sleep a lot and play computer games."

B Complete the language school brochure with the correct words.

a) accent	b) accommodation
c) examinations	d) intensive
e) host family	f) included
g) self-access	h) excursions

Welcome to Summerfield Language School!

At Summerfield School we offer all sorts of courses: long courses, short (1) ...... courses, business English, pronunciation practice to improve your English (2) ... or special courses to help you pass (3) .... We also offer an independent learning course where you can use our (4) ...... room. Summerfield's can help you with (5) ...... here. We can arrange a hotel, a stay with a (6) ...... in their own home or a flat. We can also arrange (7) ...... to places of interest. These are, however, not (8) ..... in the price of the course.

3 Use of English

Complete the second sentence so that it means the same as the first.

1 People speak English in lots of different places in the world.
   People speak English all ...... the world.
2 I'd like to speak English better.
   I'd like to ...... my English.
3 It isn't possible to have a perfect accent.
   It's ...... to have a perfect accent.
4 I've arranged to do a summer language course.
   I'm ...... a language course in the summer.

4 Pronunciation: Intonation in questions

A 🔊 Listen to these questions from the listening activity 5 in Unit 16. Does the speaker's voice rise [↗] or fall [↘]?

1 What's the best way to learn English?   [......]
2 What do you like doing?   [......]
3 How can I find a good course?   [......]
4 Why don't you come and see me later in the week?   [......]

B 🔊 Now listen to these questions. Does the speaker's voice rise [↗] or fall [↘]?

1 Do you have a minute?   [......]
2 Do you like writing?   [......]
3 Is that a good idea?   [......]
4 Would one o'clock suit you?   [......]

C Complete the intonation rules. Then listen to the questions in A and B again and repeat them.

- In **wh**-questions the speaker's voice usually ....
- In **yes / no** questions the speaker's voice usually ....

5 Portfolio Writing

A Your friend has sent you an email. He / She wants to go to the cinema on Saturday or Sunday. What Sunday is best and arrange a time and place to meet. (70–80 words).

B Write an article for your college magazine with the title 'Tips for learning English' (120–150 words).

Units 9–16 Progress check 2   Workbook   See pages 42–75

1 Language

A Complete the dialogue with *will / won't, might / might not,* or the present continuous tense.

Kate   What (1 *do*) ...... you ...... in the summer holidays?
Beth   Well, my cousin's (2 *get*) ...... married on Saturday. That definitely (3 *be*) ...... much fun; I hate weddings! Then we (4 *go*) .... camping for a few days in Scotland. I'm sure it (5 *rain*) ......, it always rains there. We (6 *travel*) ...... round a bit after that, but my parents haven't decided yet. What about you?
Kate   I (7 *do*) ...... an Italian course in Florence for the first two weeks. I love Italy, so I'm sure I (8 *enjoy*) ...... that. Then I don't know. I'd like to visit friends in London but they (9 *be*) ...... there in August. So I (10 *probably / stay*) ...... at home.

B What are you doing in the summer holidays? Write three sentences.
1 ....
2 ....
3 ....

C Your friend wants to lose weight. Tell him or her what you think he / she has to do.
1 You have to ....
2 But you don't have to ....
3 You really need to ....
4 But you don't need to ....

D Which sentences are incorrect? Correct the mistakes.
1 I haven't spoken to my sister since three weeks. ....
2 My parents were married since 1985.
3 I've been a student for two years.
4 My family live in the same house since I was born. ....
5 My brother has had his own flat for a year.
6 My grandparents have been dead since a long time. ....

E Complete the sentences.
1 If everybody has a robot in the future, ...
2 The printer won't work unless ....
3 You can take fantastic photos if ....
4 If we buy a flat screen TV, ...
5 Unless you get internet access, ...
6 People get annoyed with machines if ....

F Put the words in the correct order. Then underline the infinitives of purpose.
1 to / get / needs / a good job / to / Everybody / learn / foreign languages
2 use / many / English / to / countries / from / communicate / People / with people
3 courses / to / foreign languages / do / learn / Most people
4 English / in / A lot of people / an English-speaking country / to / stay / learn
5 listen / improve / a good idea / your accent / to / to CDs / It's / to
6 people / can use / different countries / to / You / get to know / the internet / from

G Complete the text with the past continuous or the past simple tense.

I (1 *fly*) ...... to Paris when I (2 *have*) ...... a frightening experience. We were in the air and I (3 *read*) ...... a magazine when the pilot (4 *say*) ...... we had to land. There was a problem with the engine. Suddenly everybody (5 *start*) ...... to get nervous. The flight attendant (6 *have to*) ...... hold one woman because she (7 *scream*) ...... all the time. Then while we (8 *land*) ......, the engine (9 *stop*) ...... Luckily, we (10 *land*) ...... safely. I travel everywhere by train now!

Units 9–16

Progress check 2   Workbook

2 Vocabulary

A Do the word search. Find:
1 Five illness words
2 Five special occasions
3 Five inventions

Clues: Four words like this [→]
Three words like this [↓]
Four words like this, top right to bottom left [↙]
Four words like this, bottom right to top left [↗]

```
J E N G A G E M E N T J X B L L
J P P R I N T I N G P R E S S K
M R K K P Q M K Q Q E N R G W M
V R O G R J N G T H I N L R H G
Z L M B Q F V T S C B H V A P K
M B W L O K Y A I T M H A D H G
P A B N H T W D R K T W C U Y R
K T R B M H E E W R K H C A K G
X T V K S M C K I E G M I T T Q
R E M I H N T B Y D D P N I Z L
R R D H A M W Q B Y I D E O T G
M I D C Q K Y J N G W S I N R K
D E H T P M R X X W K H E N B L
M S R V D W D D G K N M E A G D
B M A N N I V E R S A R Y E S B
Q L Q I N J E C T I O N M P L E
```

B Complete the text with the correct words from the box.

a) arrested	b) bank accounts	c) committed
d) stole	e) called	f) bank balance
g) prison	h) fraud	

In 2001, the police (1) …… James Burnett for (2) …… and he later went to (3) ……. . Over a period of six months Burnett (4) …… an amazing crime. He (5) …… hundreds of thousands of dollars from the world's richest people. How did he do it? He found out details of their (6) …… using the internet and different email addresses. Then he phoned or emailed the banks and asked them to send money to other (7) ……. . At first it worked. But one bank became worried when he asked for $10 million and (8) …… the police.

C Put the words in the correct lists.

a) drive	b) exhaust pipe	c) fare
d) flight	e) handlebars	f) steering wheel
g) pedal	h) roundabout	i) traffic lights
j) passengers	k) saddle	l) junction

Bikes	Cars

Planes	Roads

D Look at the family tree and complete the sentences.

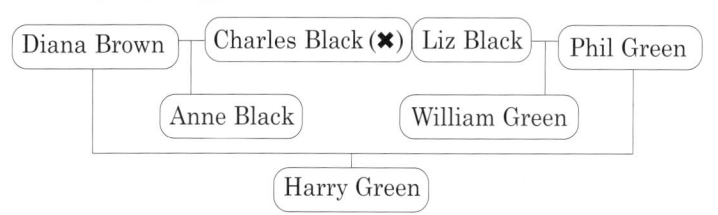

Diana Brown — Charles Black (✘) — Liz Black — Phil Green
Anne Black   William Green
Harry Green

a) divorced	b) single parent	c) daughter
d) son	e) married	f) half brother
g) cousins	h) stepmother	i) sister

Charles (1) …… Diana Brown and they had a (2) ……, Anne Black. Charles' sister Liz married Phil Green and they had a (3) ……, William Green. Anne Black and William Green are (4) ……. When Charles died, Diana became a (5) …… Later Phil and Liz got (6) …… Phil Green then married Diana Brown and they had a son, Harry Green. Harry Green is the (7) …… of William Green. Diana Brown is the (8) …… of William Green.

E Circle the odd one out of these words and phrases.

1 a) illegal   b) allowed
   c) banned   d) against the law
2 a) switch   b) socket
   c) plug   d) experiment
3 a) kilometre b) century
   c) decade   d) second
4 a) software   b) hardware
   c) data   d) laboratory
5 a) polluting   b) convenient
   c) safe   d) quick
6 a) brake   b) fly
   c) accelerate d) overtake

39

Units 1–2: Language banks

1 Talking about permanent situations and repeated actions

- We always wear knee pads.
- People often get injuries.
- We check our equipment every time.
- Surfing makes you happy.
- It's dangerous.

Answer these questions about yourself.
1 What do you always do in the morning?
2 What do you usually do in the evening?
3 What makes you happy?

2 Talking about the past and sequencing events

- What did you do on Saturday?
  - **First** I went to the park.
  - **Then** I put on this helmet.
  - **Next** I put on my knee pads.
  - **After that**, I put on my wrist guards.
  - **Finally**, I started my skateboarding. And I didn't get any injuries!

Put these events in order [2] to [9] and add three sequencing words.

[1] ..... My friend went inline skating.
[...] ..... I put my coat around him.
[...] ..... I asked for an ambulance.
[...] ..... I rang Emergency Services.
[...] ..... The ambulance came and took him to hospital.
[...] ..... I told them we were in the park.
[...] ..... I helped him to sit down.
[...] ..... I got him to support his injured foot.
[...] ..... He fell and broke his ankle.

3

Giving advice	Receiving advice
• You **should** be careful. • You **shouldn't** drink too much. • Why don't you go with your brother? • Make sure you take your phone.	• OK. / Right. • That's a good idea. • I'm not sure about that. • I don't think that's necessary / a good idea.

Damien wants to be a pop star. Complete the advice to him and add two more sentences.

1 You ..... have singing lessons.
2 ..... you learn to dance.
3 You ..... get a new look.
4 ..... you apply for one of those pop academy TV shows?
5 You ..... expect to become a star too quickly.
6 You ..... get a manager.
7 ....
8 ....

Language banks 4, 5, 6

Units 2–4

4 Describing frequency and manner

Asking about frequency	Describing frequency
• **How often** do you dance?	• Almost always • Quite often • Sometimes • Hardly ever • Never. • Once a week • Twice a month • Three times a year • Every day / week / month.

Asking about manner	Describing manner
• **How well** can you dance?	• Quite well • Really well • Perfectly • Not very well • Very badly

Complete the dialogues.

Lola   How often do you practise the drums?
Tom   1 ...I don't have time.
Lola   2 ...can you play?
Tom   Very badly!

Sam   How well can you sing?
Lisa   3 ...I sing in a band.
Sam   4 ...do you perform?
Lisa   About twice a month.

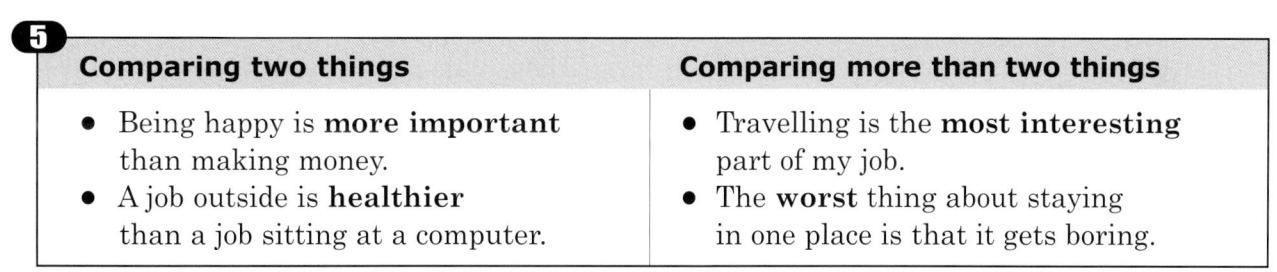

5

Comparing two things	Comparing more than two things
• Being happy is **more important** than making money. • A job outside is **healthier** than a job sitting at a computer.	• Travelling is the **most interesting** part of my job. • The **worst** thing about staying in one place is that it gets boring.

Complete the dialogues. Use the adjectives in the comparative or the superlative form.

Sales manager   This meeting is about ideas. I want only your very (1 *bright*) ...... ideas.
Chairperson   Let's sit in a circle at the round table. That's (2 *democratic*) ...... and (3 *creative*) ......
Accountant   We made some big decisions at our last meeting, but this time we have to make even (4 *important*) ...... ones.
Chairperson   OK. Then it's (5 *easy*) ...... to sit at the long table, so I can be in the in the (6 *good*) ...... place to hear everyone's opinion.

6

Asking about likes	Expressing likes and dislikes
• Do you like watching TV? • What's your favourite show?	like • Yes, I **like / love / enjoy** watching soap operas. • My **favourite / best** / TV show is... • I **don't mind** game shows but ... • No, I **don't like** going to the cinema. • I'm **not keen** on ... • I **hate** ... dislike

Complete the sentences about TV or films.

1 I love ...   2 I hate ...   3 I don't mind ... but   4 I'm not keen on ...   5 My favourite ...

Units 4–5 Language banks 7, 8, 9

7

Asking about future plans	Talking about future plans and intentions
• What are you **going to** do this evening? • What are your plans for tomorrow? • Are you **going to** …?	• I'm **going to** see a film. What about you? • I haven't got any plans. • I'm not **going to** do anything special.

Write about Lenny's plans for next week.

Monday: Take DVD back to shop
Tuesday: ……
Wednesday: Go jogging
Thursday: Watch *Survivor* on TV
Friday: ……
Saturday: Go swimming with Matt
Sunday: Write emails

1 On Monday ………………………………………………
2 ……………………………………………………………
3 ……………………………………………………………
4 ……………………………………………………………
5 ……………………………………………………………
6 ……………………………………………………………
7 ……………………………………………………………

8

Complaining			
I'm afraid this item… • … is faulty. • … doesn't work.	I'd like … • … a refund. • … to exchange it. • … to speak to the manager.	Here's my… • … receipt. • … guarantee.	• I'm not happy about that. • Thank you for your help.

Complete the dialogue:

Assistant   Can I help you?
Customer   Yes, (1) ………………………… this jacket is (2) ………………………… . Look here!
Assistant   Yes, you're right.
Customer   I'd like (3) ………………………… , please. Here's my (4) …………………………
Assistant   I'm sorry, we don't have another one in that size.
Customer   Then I'd like a (5) ………………………… .
Assistant   I'm sorry. I can't give you your money back.
Customer   Right, I (6) ………………………… to speak to the manager, please.

9

Quantifying		
• Do you like …? • Do you do (something) much?	• Yes, a lot. • A little. • No, not much. • No, not at all.	[+ +] [+] [–] [– –]

Answer the questions. Use adverbials of quantity and add more information.

For example: • Do you listen to music much?   • No, not much. I prefer watching TV.
1 Do you read much?   ………………………………………
2 Do you like staying at home?   ………………………………………
3 Do you go to museums much?   ………………………………………
4 Do you enjoy cycling?   ………………………………………

Language banks 10, 11, 12

10

Asking for reasons	Giving reasons
• **Why** do you like meat? • **What** do you eat meat **for**?	• I eat meat **because** it's good for you. • I like meat **because of** the taste. • It tastes good and it's healthy. **That's why** I like meat.

Choose statement A or B and give reasons for your choice.

1	A I eat chocolate.	B I don't eat chocolate.	1 ....
2	A I enjoy sport.	B I don't enjoy sport.	2 ....
3	A A good body is important.	B A good body isn't important.	3 ....
4	A I eat out.	B I don't eat out.	4 ....

11

Making requests	Replying to requests
• Can / Could / May I have …? • I'd like … , please. • I'll have ….	• Certainly. / Sure. / No problem. • Here you are. • Would you like …?

Complete the dialogues with phrases from Language Bank 11.

Waiter	Can I help you?
Customer	(1) ………………………… the menu, please?
Waiter	(2) ………………………… , I'll just get it. (3) ………………………… , sir.
Customer	Thank you.
	…
Waiter	Are you ready to order?
Customer	Yes, (4) ………………………… an orange juice, please. And to eat,
	(5) ………………………… the vegetable lasagne and a salad.
Waiter	(6) ………………………… bread?
Customer	Yes, please.

12

Talking about events in the indefinite past	Events in the recent past
Have you ever …? • Yes, I've done that lots of times / two or three times / …. • Yes, I did that last year / three years ago / …. • No, I've never done that / tried that.	What have you done at college recently? • Well, I've just … • Recently / Lately I've …

Complete the sentences about you.

1 I've ………………………………………………… lots of times.
2 I've ………………………………………………… two or three times.
3 I've never ………………………………………………… .
4 I've just ………………………………………………… .

Units 8–9 **Language banks** 13, 14, 15

13

Making a phone call	Answering a phone call
• Hi, it's Ellie. • Can I speak to Sam, please? • Is Sam at home? • Can you give him a message? Thanks. • See you. / Bye.	• Hello. • Just a minute. • I'm afraid he's out. • Can I take a message? • I'll tell him.

Rewrite this telephone dialogue in the correct order (1-7).

A **Lilly** Can you tell her I've got the tickets for the concert? ………
B **Dad** I'm afraid she's out, Lilly. ………
C **Lilly** Thanks, bye. ………
D **Dad** Sure. ………
E **Lilly** Oh, … er can you give her a message, please? ………
F **Dad** Yes, I'll tell her, Lilly. Thanks for calling. ………
G **Lilly** Hi, it's Lilly. Can I speak to Charlotte, please? …1…

14

Asking about preferences	Talking about preferences
• Which do you prefer, formal clothes or casual clothes? • Do you prefer going to clothes shops, or shopping online? • Which brand do you like best?	• I prefer casual clothes. • I like casual clothes better than formal clothes. • I prefer going to shops. • I like FUBU best. • My favourite brand is FUBU.

Write the questions for the answers.

1 **Matt** (Question)………………………………………………………………………… ?
  Chloe I prefer the black jacket. The blue jacket is horrible.
2 **Ryan** (Question)………………………………………………………………………… ?
  Oliver I prefer shopping in small clothes shops. I don't like going to department stores.
3 **Rosie** (Question)………………………………………………………………………… ?
  Lucy I like Stella McCartney best. I think she's a really interesting designer.

15

Expressing obligation and necessity		
• What do you have to do at home? • Do you have to cook / go shopping / do housework?	• I have to / must … • It's my job to … • I don't have to … .	• I need to … because … • I don't need to … . • It's my turn to … .

Complete the dialogue.

Laura (1) ……… you ……… do anything special at home this weekend?
Christina I (2) ……… help my mum with Dad's birthday meal on Sunday. It's (3) ……… to make the dessert.
Laura (4) ……… you ……… stay at home all day Sunday?
Christina Yeah, I think so.
Laura That's too bad. I (5) ……… do anything at home this weekend because my parents are away. But I (6) ……… go to town tomorrow to buy Suzie a present.
Christina You (7) ……… to buy her a present. You can just burn a CD or something.
Laura I know, but it's (8) ……… to get her something. You got her a present last time.

Language banks 16, 17, 18

16

Giving instructions	Following instructions
• First plug that cable in there. • Then switch it on. • Choose the programme. • You need to … • Remember to …	• OK. / Right. / Ah, I see. • What do I do next? • I don't understand that. • Can you say that again? • It doesn't work.

Rewrite this dialogue in the correct order (1–8).

A	David	Er, Holly. Remember to put the DVD in the player.	………
B	Holly	Oh. I've done that! What do I do next?	………
C	Holly	But nothing is happening.	………
D	David	It means plug the cable in and switch it on at the socket.	………
E	David	Then just switch it on and press 'play'. That's not difficult.	………
F	Holly	Oh no, the new DVD player doesn't work!	…1…
G	Holly	What? I don't understand that.	………
H	David	Let me see the instructions. It says here 'First connect to the mains'.	………

17

Informing about the future	Predicting the future
• What do you think will happen in the future? • What will happen in the next decade / century? • What do you think your life will be like in …? • Do you think you'll… ?	• I think there'll be / we'll … • It's possible that … will … • I don't think that …will … • I think I'll … / I won't … • I think so. / I don't think so. • Maybe, / Probably, / Definitely.

Complete the conversation with the correct words or phrases.

Dave What do you think your life (1) ………… in ten years?
Jane I think I (2) ………… children. I want to have children soon. What about you?
Dave No, I don't (3) …………. I don't like children.
Jane Do you think you'll still be in England?
Dave (4)………. I can't really imagine moving.
Jane Really? I definitely (5) ……… here in ten years. I want to live abroad.

18

Asking about duration	Stating the duration of events
• How long have you …?	• For a long time / for ages / for as long as I can remember. • Since 2000 / last year / I was a child.

Answer the questions about you.

1 How long have you known your best friends?
2 How long have you had your mobile phone?
3 How long have you been interested in your favourite hobby?
4 How long have you liked your favourite food?

Units 12–13 Language banks 19, 20, 21

19

When you use telephone banking	What the bank assistant says
• Hello. My name is David **Montague**. I'd like to check my bank balance, please.	• Can you spell your second name, please?
• M-O-N-T-A-G-U-E.	• What's your account number?
• 1599-763892.	• And what's your mother's maiden name, please?
• Jones	• Thank you. Can you confirm your address, please?
• 19 Parliament Street, London N18 4BY.	• Thank you. Your balance is forty-nine pounds and fifteen pence.
• Thank you. Goodbye.	• Thank you for using Telebank.

Complete the dialogue with the correct words. Read it with a partner.

Anna Hello, I'd like to (1) …… my bank balance, please.
Assistant Certainly, What's your (2) …?
Anna Oh sorry, Anna Worthington.
Assistant Worthington? Can you (3) …… that please?
Anna W-O-R-T-H-I-N-G-T-O-N.
Assistant Right. I need your (4) ……, please.
Anna BQZ07.
Assistant Thank you. Can you (5) …… your address?
Anna 67 Newton Road, Doncaster, DN4 6GP.
Assistant Thank you. Your (6) …… is two hundred and ten pounds and twenty pence.

20

Expressing certainty	Expressing uncertainty
• Do you think people will get richer?	
• Yes. Of course people will get richer. • No, people won't get richer. • Definitely not! Not a chance! • Certainly. / Certainly not. • Probably. / Probably not.	• I think so. / I don't think so. • People might get richer. • I'm not sure. • I don't know. We'll see. • Possibly. / Possibly not.

Write answers to these questions. Then compare them with a partner.
In future, do you think …
1 you'll earn a lot of money?
2 we'll all be millionaires?
3 you'll buy your own house?
4 we won't use cash at all?

21

Expressing intention	Expressing purpose
• What do you intend to do when …? • I want to / I'd like to … • I'm going to … • I plan to / intend to … because …	• What's the purpose of …? • The point / idea is to … • It's to … • … in order to … / …so that I can …

Answer the questions.
1 What are you going to do when you've finished this exercise?
2 What's the purpose of this exercise?
3 What's the point in studying?
4 What do you intend to do at the weekend?

Language banks 22, 23, 24

22

Asking about past activities	Describing past activities
• What were you doing at 8 pm yesterday? • What were you doing on Saturday evening?	• I was having a shower. • I was watching a film at the cinema. • I was watching TV all night. • I was practising the guitar. • My sister and I were trying on clothes.

Write answers to the two questions in Language Bank 22.

1 ....

2 ....

23

Asking about past events	Describing events in the past
• What was your sister's graduation like? • Tell me about it.	• The sun was shining. / It was raining. • I was wearing … • Everyone was enjoying themselves. • While we were waiting, we …
• What happened then?	• My sister walked onto the stage. • She got her degree certificate.
• Did you enjoy it?	• It was fantastic / exciting / very enjoyable… • It was boring / terrible / upsetting / …

Complete the dialogue. Use your imagination!

Friend   What was your brother's wedding like?
You   The weather was (1) .... It (2) ....
          I was wearing (3) ....
          The best part was when (4) ....
          The worst part was when (5) ....
Friend   Did you enjoy it?
You   (6) ....

24

Talking about facts

- The fact is, bird flu is very infectious.
- The problem is, people don't want to kill birds.
- If people get bird flu, they can die.
- As far as bird flu is concerned, people need to be very careful.

You are talking about smoking. Complete the sentences.

1 The fact is ....
2 The problem is ....
3 If people smoke, ...
4 As far as passive smoking is concerned, ...

Units 15–16: Language banks — 25, 26, 27

25

Requesting opinions and impressions	Expressing opinions and impressions
• What do you think of …? • What's your opinion of …?	• I think … / I don't think … • I reckon… / I don't reckon … • In my opinion, … / In my view, …
• What's your impression of …? • How do you feel about …?	• If you ask me, … • My impression is … • It seems to me that…

Answer these questions.
1 What do you think of medical progress?
2 What's your opinion of your doctor?
3 What's your impression of how your country deals with health problems?
4 How do you feel about giving money to poor countries to fight disease?

26

Making arrangements	
• What are you doing in the holidays?	• I'm going to …
• Would you like to … next week?	• That's a good idea. • Thanks, that would be great.
• Why don't we … tomorrow?	• I'm afraid I'm … . • Sorry, I already have other plans.
• What day / time would suit you?	• Can we say Saturday? • How about 7 o'clock?
• What about Sunday at 8 o'clock? • Let's meet at … .	• That's fine.
• I'm free on …	• … would be better.
• OK. See you then.	

Complete the telephone conversation.
Carrie Hi Anna, it's Carrie. Listen, (1) …… play tennis on Saturday?
Anna Oh, I'm (2) ……… I'm going on an excursion with my parents.
Carrie OK. What (3) …… on Sunday?
Anna Sorry, I already have plans for Sunday. But (4) …… we play tennis on Friday?
Carrie That's a good idea. What time (5) ……… you?
Anna Can we say 4 o'clock at the sports centre?
Carrie That's fine. (6) …….. then.

27

Talking about future arrangements	Talking about future intentions
• Tonight I'm going out with Beth. • We're having dinner together. • We've arranged to meet Sam later.	• Tonight I'm going to stay at home. • I'm going to watch TV. • I plan to / intend to go to bed early.

Write about your arrangements and intentions for tomorrow.
1 ………………………………………………………………………………………………
2 ………………………………………………………………………………………………

Unit 1   Adrenalin rush

CD 1, Track 1 (*American English*)
Tim: You went skydiving? Are you crazy? That's dangerous!
Alicia: Oh, don't worry! First I did a jump with my instructor. I put on a protective suit, a helmet for my head and goggles for my eyes. Then my instructor tied me to his parachute. We jumped out of the plane together and screamed. That helped us to keep breathing normally. Later I did jumps by myself.
Tim: Well, I think it's wrong to do those dangerous sports.
Alicia: Come on! We're not kids, are we? And it's such a great feeling.
Tim: Weren't you scared?
Alicia: Of course I was! But I did it, that's the great thing. You're in the open door of the plane, really, really scared… And the next minute you're out in the air, flying at 200 kilometres per hour…. What an adrenalin rush! And afterwards you say, 'YES, I did it'!
Tim: People die doing extreme sports. What's wrong with ordinary sports, like soccer?
Alicia: Boring…soccer is so boring. You just run around on a field in the rain.
Tim: Right, but you get to work with others in a team. That's got to be good.
Alicia: Well, I don't want that. I want to do something by myself. You don't know what skydiving feels like. Come with me next week.
Tim: No way! Give me our soccer team any day. It's safe, it's good exercise; I'm with my friends.
Alicia: Well, lots of kids have accidents in school sports, too. In fact, most accidents happen in traditional sports.
Tim: That's because people don't wear any protection.
Alicia: Didn't you sprain your ankle playing football last week?
Tim: At least I didn't die!
Alicia: Well, for me, it's the danger that makes a sport really thrilling.
Tim: Thrilling, hah! I just want to stay alive – even if I can't walk on my sprained ankle.

Unit 2   Carnival atmosphere

CD 1, Track 2 (*London English*)
Reporter: Hello. I'm Corinna Jones and I'm reporting from this year's Notting Hill Carnival in London. As usual the news is full of problems at the Carnival. So, what do people in the crowd think? Excuse me, Madam, what do you think of the Carnival?
Woman: Well, the young people dancing, the food, the floats and the costumes are wonderful but … well, Carnival is really too big now. There are too many tourists; it isn't OUR Carnival any more. And it isn't safe. Some people here have got knives and when they're drunk, there can be violence. There's too much alcohol. And everyone knows you can get drugs at the Carnival.
Reporter: But there are thousands of police officers here.
Woman: Huh. The police are just here to dance. The organizers don't want to spoil the image of the Carnival as a nice multicultural festival. The Carnival makes a lot of money from sponsors, you know.
Reporter: OK, thanks. Let's get another opinion. Excuse me.
Man: Yeah?
Reporter: What do you think of the music? There seem to be even louder sound systems, more DJs and more hip-hop music here today than in the past.
Man: Yeah, well, the Carnival's over 40 years old now and the music needs to change with the times. The traditional Caribbean carnival had steel bands and calypso music. There are still a few steel bands, but I guess it's the London Carnival now. It's for everyone and that means different types of music – hip hop, soul, jazz, reggae, everything.
Reporter: Do you think the Carnival's too commercial?
Man: Yes, it is – but everything's commercial nowadays. Festivals like this can't survive without sponsorship. But just look around you – it's still a great Carnival where you can dance and have a good time and that's the most important thing. Sometimes people do drink too much, but it's actually quite safe.

Unit 3   Lifestyle choices

CD 1, Track 3 (*British*)
Gary: What jobs did you find most interesting, Lynn?
Lynn: Well, I thought maybe … accountancy… or working as a financial analyst with one of the big banks…
Gary: Really? Oh man, those jobs are for geeks - so boring! You want to work with numbers and computers ALL DAY LONG?

Units 3–6 Audio texts CD 1 Listening

Lynn: I love numbers. My best subject is maths, remember? I'm a techie – I love all that IT stuff. The technology gets more amazing all the time.
Gary: But it's a life full of stress. You've got to be in the office from 8 to 5 or even later every day. All those meetings …. How boring is that!
Lynn: Well OK, boring for you, but I like having a steady routine. It's a secure job. And I can get promotion.
Gary: C'mon. You sound just like my Dad! I want more adventure in my life. I want a challenge, more variety… that's better than routine and promotion!
Lynn: What kind of job do you want, then?
Gary: I don't know, really. I thought erm…something in the media…you know, maybe I'd like to be a freelance reporter, or a news photographer…
Lynn: What a horrible idea! You go to all those terrible disasters, and wars… and accidents….It's dangerous. You spend all your time travelling…. that's the worst thing I can think of.
Gary: Why? You get to see other countries; you're working with great people. It's a real adventure… You've got to admit, it's more fun than sitting at a computer all day.
Lynn: Not for me, it isn't. When I'm working on my computer, that's when I'm happiest! I'm always learning new things. I prefer a steady job in an office, thank you very much.
Gary: And a good salary, and a car, I bet.
Lynn: Yeah, why not? Money doesn't give you happiness….but it certainly helps!

Unit 3 Lifestyle choices
CD 1, Track 4 (*British*)
Pronunciation: Vowels (*See Workbook page 9*)
A Some vowel sounds in English can have different spellings:

ship (1)	sheep (2)	get (3)

B Now listen to the sentences and check the answers you gave in A.
- My friend's a ski instructor – he teaches winter sports and spends his life in a cleaner and healthier environment.
- The garden centre specialist likes having her own business, meeting people, and not having a routine.

Unit 4 Stranger than fiction
CD 1, Track 5 (*American*)
Speaker 1: I love all the reality shows. I'm going to watch *Beautiful People* tonight – that program where they take an unattractive woman and give her plastic surgery so she looks like a beauty queen. I think it's amazing. They're, like, just normal women like me and then afterwards they're so beautiful. The women are so brave, too. I mean the operations are painful and they can't look in a mirror for, like, four months. I'd love to be on a show like that and be famous, but my boyfriend says, 'no way'.
Speaker 2: Tonight I'm going to watch *Your Date*. A girl goes on eight blind dates – you know, she doesn't know the men at all. Then each week she says goodbye to one, and in the last show she chooses which man she wants to marry. It's great! I like reality shows. Some are really dumb, though. I watched this girl on a show last night and she cried because she had to eat worms. But I mean, she wanted to go on that program. These people go on game shows for the money and the fame; it's their own fault if they can't cope with the problems.
Speaker 3: I'm not going to watch TV tonight. I don't watch TV much, especially all those reality shows. Man, those programs suck! Those stupid women in the makeover shows think they can change their appearance and everyone will love them. These shows just exploit and humiliate people – like that *I Wanna Be a Star* program where people want to be pop stars. Most of them can't sing at all and they cry when the judges tell them how bad they are. It's awful. The producers plan a lot of what happens on these reality shows, you know. It's not as real as you think!

Unit 4 Stranger than fiction
CD 1, Track 6 (*British*)
Pronunciation: Consonants
(*See Workbook page 11*)
A 1 Listen to these pairs of words. Can you hear the difference?

fewer	viewer
came	game

B 1 Listen and circle the word you hear.

A		dead
B		very
C	sink	
D		bit
E	class	
F	choke	

Unit 5 Shopaholics
CD 1, Track 7 (*American*)
Debbie: Hello, Super Smart Customer Services, Debbie speaking. How can I help you?
Lucy: Hello. I ordered some gifts last week from your website, but the delivery is completely wrong!
Debbie: Oh dear! What's your name, please?
Lucy: Lucy Smith.
Debbie: Lucy Smith, ah, yes … right, what's the problem, Lucy?
Lucy: Well, firstly, I ordered a Robbie Williams CD and I got a Coldplay CD.
Debbie: Really? I'm sorry about that. But I can really recommend Coldplay – they're brilliant!
Lucy: Yes, but … I also ordered a black backpack, and I received a pink handbag.
Debbie: Oh … Well, pink is THE colour right now, isn't it? I have a pink handbag myself.
Lucy: Yes, but it's my brother's birthday present. I don't think my brother wants a pink handbag for his birthday! Listen, the order is wrong! Some things are missing, too. I'd like to speak to the manager, please.
Debbie: Oh, I'm sorry he's on his lunch break right now. …Did you get our free gift? … The Super Smart shopping bag?
Lucy: Oh, yes I did. You can have it back! It's faulty. There's a hole in it!
Debbie: Well, we can exchange that, no problem! I'll send a new one out to you in Manchester.
Lucy: Manchester? I live in Brighton!
Debbie: I'm sorry – Aren't you Lucy Smith of 21 Wellington Gardens, Manchester?
Lucy: No, I'm not. I mean, I am Lucy Smith, but I live at 33 Aintree Avenue, Brighton.
Debbie: Oh, dear. That's why you got the wrong order! Just a minute … The correct order is on its way to you right now, Lucy!
Lucy: But what about these other things?
Debbie: Please keep them. That CD is really very good! Thank you for calling. Have a nice day!
Lucy: Well!

Unit 6 Eat your greens!
CD 1, Track 8 (*American*)
Ellen: What time is it? I'm hungry!
Dan: Me, too! Let's get a cheeseburger.
Ellen: Erm, well, actually, I don't eat burgers any more.
Dan: What??
Ellen: I decided to become a vegetarian last weekend. It's healthier.
Dan: Oh, Ellen, that's crazy! Vegetarians are always thin and unhealthy. You don't get enough iron and vitamins without meat.
Ellen: You can get iron and vitamins from other foods.
Dan: But vegetarian food is so bland and boring. People need meat!
Ellen: That's not true. And what about the poor animals?
Dan: Well, they're only animals aren't they? Humans are more important than animals.
Ellen: No! Animals …
Dan: What about the vegetables? It's cruel to kill plants, too! And look at all the GM crops now. Tomatoes with fish genes and potatoes with chicken genes, for example. That's not healthy, is it?
Ellen: No, but … but people in lots of countries are hungry and producing meat takes away the land they need to grow their food.
Dan: Well, I don't care about people in other countries. Farmers in this country need jobs! Besides, I'm hungry now and I need meat. It tastes better than other things and I don't care where it comes from! It's about freedom of choice, isn't it?
Ellen: Yes, it is – and I choose not to eat meat.
Dan: Ellen … Let's order. Do you want a boring vegetarian salad?
Ellen: No, thanks. I'm not hungry now.
Dan: OK. … A half pound triple cheeseburger and fries, please.
Assistant: Sure. What would you like to drink?
Dan: Nothing, thanks.
Assistant: That's ten dollars ninety-five, please. Here you are. Thank you. Have a nice day!
Dan: Thanks. Mmm… delicious! You can't beat meat!

Unit 6 Eat your greens!
CD 1, Track 9 (*American*)
Pronunciation: Word stress
(*See Workbook page 15*)
A 1 Listen to and repeat these nouns and adjectives.

environment	environmental
accident	accidental
misery	miserable
knowledge	knowledgeable
geography	geographic
economy	economic

Units 6–10 Audio texts — CD 1 — Listening

B 1 Listen and repeat.

pro**duce**	**pro**duce
in**crease**	**in**crease
de**crease**	**de**crease
ex**port**	**ex**port
re**search**	**re**search

Unit 7 For your eyes only
CD 1, Track 10 (*American*)
Lizzie: I can't believe you've done that! You've posted stuff about me on your website! What did you do that for?
Josh: Why not? I love you, Lizzie, and I want to tell people how I feel! It's not a secret, is it?
Lizzie: It's just self-exposure, that's what it is. I want our lives to be private, thank you very much. I don't want you writing stuff about me on the web, so everybody in the whole wide world can read it.
Josh: Well, I've never written anything bad. In fact, I've only said how smart, how GREAT you are. You're the best thing that's ever happened to me. Why can't I tell other people that?
Lizzie: Typical! You men are so self-centred. You don't think about other people's feelings.
Josh: Oh, come on, that's not fair, Lizzie. You know it's not just men who write blogs. There are lots of web diaries by women. And some of them write about everything in their lives. And I mean everything! But then that's the great thing about blogs – you can write about *anything*. There's no control.
Lizzie: Well, you've got no self-control. Most blogs are just boring stuff anyway. There are no editors to check that people write about something interesting – or that they write properly. Have you noticed how many people can't even spell?
Josh: Yeah, OK … but if you don't want to read blogs, just don't read them. I think they're a good way to find out about other people's experiences and, you know, meet new people.
Lizzie: Meet new people'? How can you do that on a computer? That's not real communication. You know, I think we all just spend too much time on the internet – and too little time talking to our friends and family.
Josh: Give me a break! The internet is a great way to communicate, can't you see that?

Unit 7 For your eyes only
CD 1, Track 11 (*British*)
Pronunciation: Strong and weak forms
(*See Workbook page 17*)
A Listen and repeat these sentences.
 1 Writers post details about their lives **and** thoughts.
 2 Sam has just proposed **to** me.
 3 I write without **an** editor changing things.
 4 Here are some tips **for** writers.
B Listen and repeat these sentences.
 1 This blog isn't just about me – it's about me **and** you.
 2 I had nobody to talk **to**.
 3 He hasn't just got **an** editor, he's got three!
 4 What did you do that **for**?
C Listen and check your answers.
 1 I wrote about it in my blog, **of** course.
 2 Where does Salam Pax come **from**?
 3 She's **at** her desk.
 4 I'm not **as** clever as you – I'm cleverer!

Unit 8 Fashionistas
CD 1, Track 12 (*British, Australian, South African*)
Man: Hello. I'm from your mobile phone company. We're doing a survey, asking people how they use their mobile phones.
Martin: Oh, hello…. right. Well, I use mine for calls sometimes, but that's too expensive. I prefer sending text messages. My girlfriend and I text all the time. I also use it for playing games, mostly when I'm on the bus, or in the breaks at college.
Lindy: I've got two mobiles. I use them to chat with friends. We don't really talk about anything important – you know, just what's happening, and who's seeing who.
Excuse me…
Oh … Hi Em, where are you?
Listen, I'm on the other line. Can you call me back in a minute? Bye.
Yeah, as I was saying …..
Erica: For me, it's really important how my mobile looks. It's really small and very stylish. I have three different covers for it, so it always matches my look.
Thomas: I've just got a job with a sales company and they gave me a mobile. I'm out in the car a lot, but I'm careful not to use it while driving. I use it to check my email and call customers.
Mike: If you don't text, you're out of it. I use texts to ask girls out. Once I used a text to dump a girlfriend, but everyone said that was a horrible

thing to do. Oh, and my mobile's really useful for watching the latest football goals.
Roz: I love my mobile! My boyfriend works away from home a lot, so we send video messages to each other. I don't miss him as much when I can see where he is and what he's doing. Sometimes I download music and listen to it on my phone. But I don't think the quality's very good. I've got a really good MP3 player, so I prefer using that.
Message: Hi. I can't take your call now. Please leave a message after the beep.

Unit 9   Rule of law

CD 1, Track 13 (*British*)
Jim: Welcome to the programme. Today Jeremy Parsons, the author of a new book called *Banned by Law,* is here to tell us about some new rules and laws.
Jeremy: Hi, Jim. Thanks for allowing me to be here!
Jim: So far, there's no law against it, Jeremy! Let's start with New York. The mayor has tried to clean up the city, hasn't he?
Jeremy: That's right. It's now illegal to drink alcohol in public places, or smoke in restaurants. And it's illegal to feed the pigeons!
Jim: Presumably a lot of people are angry about the bans.
Jeremy: Well, New York is now a nicer place to live. But people want to make their own decisions; they don't want to follow so many rules.
Jim: Yes, it's all about individual freedom, or government control, isn't it? What about the rest of the world?
Jeremy: Well, In Tokyo you mustn't use your mobile phone on the train.
Jim: That's seems fair enough.
Jeremy: Well, yes, but here's a strange one from Halifax, Canada. People there aren't allowed to wear perfume, or other products that have a strong smell.
Jim: What?
Jeremy: Yes, apparently some people become ill when they smell perfume. Police arrested a 17-year-old boy because he wore hair gel at college!
Jim: Well, that's going a bit far ... You've also got an example of a ban on English words. What's that about?
Jeremy: Well, the French government thinks that people use too many English words. They tried to ban the word 'email', for example – people have to use the French expression 'courier electronique' instead.

Jim: That's really convenient! Does it work?
Jeremy: Not really.
Jim: Mmm, right. Let's move on to some of the silliest laws.
Jeremy: Well, there are lots of silly laws. The one I like is the ban on gold teeth by the president of Turkmenistan.
Jim: Gold teeth?
Jeremy: Yes, the president thinks white teeth look much better!
Jim: Well, that's a good reason for a law!

Unit 9   Rule of law

CD 1, Track 14 (*British*)
Pronunciation: Stress on auxiliary verbs
(*See Workbook page 23*)
A Listen and mark the stressed verbs.
  1 I can **phone** her on my mobile.
  2 Do you **smoke**?
  3 You **must** remember to wash your hands.
  4 Those people are **breaking** the law.
  5 Excuse me, I **need** to get out here.
B Listen and repeat these sentences.
  1 Oh no! Look at the room. What **have** you done?
  2 We don't have a choice, we **must** call the police.
  3 I **can't** do it!
  4 You **can** do it if you really try.
  5 Please, I **need** to speak to him now!
  6 Let's stay a bit longer, we don't **have to** leave now.

Unit 10   What's next?

CD 1, Track 15 (*American*)
Dad: Switch on and ... oh no!
Leo: What are you doing, Dad?
Dad: I'm setting up the new computer and printer. I've plugged in all the cables, but it won't work.
Leo: Well, they will work if you've done everything properly. Let me have a look at the instruction manual.
Hmm, plug the printer cable into the USB port.
Dad: I've done that!
Leo: Plug this monitor cable into this socket.
Dad: I've done that, too! ... I hate all this technology. Life was much simpler before we had computers and dishwashers and videos. Everything is always going wrong. I'm always reading instruction books and finding people to fix things. All these machines don't

save time; they just cause problems. And things will get worse in the future!

Leo: Don't be stupid, Dad. You can't put the clock back or stop progress. You love your flat screen TV and your new car. Besides, things will be even better in the future. We won't have computers like this with cables everywhere. Everything will be wireless very soon – in fact, it is already. And soon we won't have computers on a desk at all. You'll use the computer in your watch, or even in your clothes and we'll read books on cell phones.

Dad: Yeah, yeah, I know. You're right, we can't stop progress. But technology isn't always a good thing. I mean, you teenagers don't do so many of the simple things in life … going for walks, reading books and newspapers, talking to friends … Why, when I was a boy …

Leo: Oh, Dad, don't start again. Technology gives us lots of new possibilities. I love reading books and newspapers – I just read them online, instead. And I talk to my friends; it's just easier to phone or text them sometimes.

Dad: Easier? Our house is a technological disaster!

Leo: Er, Dad, this problem has nothing to do with technology. It's a human mistake. You forgot to plug the computer into the power socket and switch it on!

Unit 11   Travel costs

CD 1, Track 16 (*English, Scottish*)

Nick: Hi, Angus! I've just booked a weekend trip to London. It only cost £32, including airport tax! Much cheaper than the train! … What's the matter?

Angus: Well, that's great but it's scary how much pollution planes produce.

Nick: Oh no, don't start about the environment again, Angus. Cheap air travel means people can see new places. Travel broadens the mind and all that … And London, Angus! I've wanted to go there for ages! Think of the clubs!

Angus: Yes, I haven't been there for years – since I was very young. It's a fantastic city. … Listen, Nick, I wanted to tell you about some special tree-planting programmes.

Nick: Tree planting? What does that have to do with my trip to London?

Angus: Well, you know trees take in carbon dioxide, don't you?

Nick: Do they? Er, I mean, er of course I know that! We did that at school.

Angus: People have planted millions of trees since they started to worry about global warming.

Nick: Er … great, but so what?

Angus: Well, lots of new trees mean less carbon dioxide in the air. And everyone can help! Using a website, you can calculate how much carbon dioxide your flights produce. Then you can find out how many trees you must plant.

Nick: I'm not sure I'm with you.

Angus: Well, for example, …er let me look on the internet. Your flight from Edinburgh to London will produce 0.12 tonnes of carbon dioxide – that's for each person, of course. So you need to plant one tree.

Nick: Mmm. … So, OK, I'm causing pollution. But is planting trees the best way to help? And anyway, it's the government's job to plant trees, isn't it? They get taxes for things like that.

Angus: Yes, but the government is too slow. We've waited for years for the government to do something. And these programmes are really popular. Lots of celebrities – people like Kylie Minogue, Leonardo Di Caprio and Dido – have planted trees.

Nick: Well, they can afford it! I'm a student, and I can't!

Unit 11   Travel costs

CD 1, Track 17 (*British*)

Pronunciation: Consonant clusters 1

(*See Workbook page 27*)

A Listen to these words and repeat.
1 **st**op, **st**udent, **st**ress
2 **sp**eak, **sp**ecial, **sp**read
3 **sl**ow, **sl**im, **sl**eep
4 **sm**all, **sm**ile, **sm**oke
5 **Sc**otland, **sc**ary, **sc**ream

B Listen and complete the words with the correct consonants.
1 **sm**art
2 **st**reet
3 **sp**end
4 **sl**edge
5 **scr**een
6 **sm**ell
7 **spr**ing
8 **st**ar

C Listen and repeat these sentences.
1 Smart students from Scotland stop smoking.
2 Special stars smile on screen.

Audio texts

Units 10–13

Unit 12 Money, money, money
CD 1, Track 18 (*British*)
Kirsty: Hi, Leanne.
Leanne: Hi Kirsty. Did you bring your magazine for me?
Kirsty: Yeah, I've got it. There's an interesting quiz about honesty this week.
Leanne: Great, I love quizzes. Let's do it now. You can read the questions to me while I'm getting ready.
Kirsty: OK, let me find it. Right, first question. You find a wallet with £30 in the street. Do you a) take it to the police or b) keep it.
Leanne: Well, er, it's only thirty pounds and nobody will know. Keep it.
Kirsty: Really? OK, b).
Right, number 2. You have a part-time job in an office. Most other people there take paper and pens home. Do you a) not do it, because it's dishonest, or b) do it, too: the company won't miss a few things.
Leanne: Mmm. I don't know. I might … But er … no, it is dishonest. And they might catch me.
Kirsty: No? So a), then. Number 3. You get too much change in your local shop. Do you a) correct the mistake and give back the extra money, or b) don't say anything and keep the money.
Leanne: Well, they work really hard in our local shop. Definitely a).
Kirsty: 3 a). … OK, number 4. The check-out assistant in a big supermarket gives you a £20 note instead of £10. Do you a) give back the extra money, or b) don't say anything and keep the money.
Leanne: Hmm, those supermarkets make millions, don't they? Keep the money, I think.
Kirsty: OK, 4 b). Last question, number 5. The bank has made a mistake. You have £1,000 too much in your account. Do you a) tell the bank immediately, or b) wait and see what happens.
Leanne: Oh, I'm not sure. … The bank might not notice the mistake. … But they always notice those mistakes sooner or later, don't they? So, I think a), tell them.
Kirsty: 5 a). OK, let me see. … that's three a)'s and two b)'s. Mmm, the magazine says: "You're quite honest – but only in some situations. Remember: taking something that isn't yours is always stealing."

Unit 13 Destination disaster
CD 1, Track 19 (*British*)
Presenter: Hello and welcome to *Discussion Time*. Today our topic is: *Cars – do we really need them?*
Here with me is Graham Long from the anti-car group *Streets 4 Us*.
Graham: Hello.
Presenter: Helen Vale from Pro Car, the car drivers' organisation.
Helen: Hello.
Presenter: Deborah Allen, a mother of four children.
Deborah: Hello.
Presenter: And Alex Reed, a new driver.
Alex: Hi.
Presenter: Let's start with you, Alex. You've just passed your driving test. Do you enjoy driving?
Alex: Yeah, I love the freedom. I can go anywhere I want. I often just drive around really fast with loud music on. And a car is a great way to get a girlfriend! Girls think cars are cool.
Presenter: What do you say to that, Deborah?
Deborah: Well, I suppose a lot of teenage drivers think like that. But when you're younger, you don't really need a car. You can use a bike to get around – it's much healthier. But I've got four children. I have to take them to school, to the doctor, to football matches, or to town to see my mum. I spend half my day in the car and I hate it – traffic jams everywhere, aggressive male drivers. But I need my car to transport the children.
Presenter: Graham, *Streets 4 Us* wants to get cars off the streets. How exactly do you intend to do that? And what about people like Deborah?
Graham: It won't be easy, but we do need to take action. Think how much space cars use in our towns. Cars need roads, petrol stations, garages, car parks … someone calculated that these things take up 23% of the total space in London, 29% in Tokyo and 44% in Los Angeles! What about space for parks and places for children to play?
Presenter: Helen, I can see you want to say something!
Helen: I just want to say 'rubbish'! How does Graham Long think we can live in today's world without cars? His organisation is just one of those silly groups that are making life harder for drivers. That's why we've got such high taxes on everything to do with cars and no parking anywhere … it makes me so angry …

55

Units 13-16 Audio texts CD 2 Listening

Unit 13 Destination disaster
CD 1, Track 20 (*British*)
Pronunciation: Consonant clusters 2
(*See Workbook page 31*)

A Listen to these words and repeat them.
1 fa**st**, cycli**st**
2 acci**de**nt, importa**nt**
3 behi**nd**, girlfrie**nd**
4 thi**nk**, ta**nk**
5 a**sk**, de**sk**

B Listen and complete the words with the correct consonants.
1 pa**st**
2 spe**nd**
3 di**sk**
4 fro**nt**
5 ba**nk**
6 inte**nd**
7 te**st**
8 sou**nd**

C Listen and repeat these sentences.
1 Fast cyclists have accidents.
2 My girlfriend intends to take her test.

Unit 14 All in the family
CD 1, Track 21 (*British*)
Emma: Hi Mum. Happy silver wedding anniversary!
Andy: Hello Miriam. Congratulations!
Mum: Hi Emma, love. Hello Andy. Thank goodness you've arrived. The guests will be here soon. Can you help?
Emma: Where's Dad?
Mum: Well, a minute ago, he was watching TV – as usual. I don't know how we've stayed married for 25 years!
Emma: Oh, Dad and TV! Guess what, Andy? Mum says Dad was late for their wedding because he was watching the football!
Mum: He was watching the World Cup at his best man's house and forgot the time! He only stops watching TV when its time to eat his dinner – the dinner that I've cooked, of course. He hasn't cooked more than five meals in 25 years!
Emma: Yes, Mum, but you still love him!
Mum: Meeting your dad was the most important event in my life. He's a great man, just a lazy husband!
Andy: Oh, I'm sure Ken does *something* in the house.
Mum: Well, I do the shopping, the cooking, the cleaning and the washing. I even do all the painting and decorating. It's just not fair when I have a full time job as well. Women are still unpaid slaves at home!
Andy: Things are changing, Miriam. Today we're all New Men. Most of us cook, help in the house and look after the children nowadays.
Emma: What? You never clean our flat. And you don't even know how the washing machine works!
Andy: Well, OK, but I often do the cooking, the washing up and the shopping. And remember I did the ironing while you were out clubbing with your friends last night.
Emma: Yes, but ….
Dad: Hello Emma. All right Andy? Where's my wonderful wife? I can't believe we got married 25 years ago. I was just thinking about our wedding … and thinking you don't look a day older, my love!
Mum: Oh, Ken …

Unit 14 All in the family
CD 1, Track 22 (*British*)
Pronunciation: Intonation in statements
(*See Workbook page 33*)

A Listen to these statements from the listening activity 5 in Unit 14.
Does the speaker's voice rise or fall?
1 The guests will be here soon.
2 He was watching sport on TV.
3 He hasn't cooked more than five meals in twenty-five years.
4 I did the ironing last night.

B Now listen to these statements. Does the speaker's voice rise or fall? Why?
1 The guests will be here in five minutes.
2 He's on the phone.
3 She's making pasta.
4 You did the washing yesterday.

C Listen to these sentences. Is the speaker certain or uncertain?
1 She's sixteen years old.
2 He's very unhappy.
3 He's an only child.
4 Their wedding's in two weeks.

Unit 15 The new epidemics
CD 1, Track 23 (*American*)
Vanessa: Hi Jake, how are you feeling?
Jake: Oh, terrible, Vanessa. I think I'm going to die.

Vanessa: Oh, come on, don't exaggerate – you've only got a cold!
Jake: It isn't just a cold, it's definitely the flu; it might even be pneumonia!
Vanessa: Yeah, right. If you just sit around and feel sorry for yourself, you'll never get better. What about going for a walk? If you get some exercise and fresh air, you'll feel fine.
Jake: Oh no, I'm too sick. I think I need some antibiotics.
Vanessa: The fact is, Jake, you're just a hypochondriac. Think of all the people who really are sick! People with AIDS or cancer. A lot of them are going to die and they can't do anything about it.
Jake: Yeah, I know, I know. And I think it's just awful. But what if I've got this bird flu that's always in the news? Everybody's saying there's going to be an epidemic soon. … Remember that terrible SARS epidemic? You know if you wear a mask, it protects you against infection. I might buy one.
Vanessa: You're not serious! … Oh, you are. Sorry, but I don't think protection is really necessary. The flu epidemic might never happen. Why should we worry about things if they aren't certain? I read that the government has bought lots of expensive drugs, so if we have a flu epidemic, we'll be OK. That's ridiculous! There are lots of people in the world who need drugs for ordinary diseases right now.
Jake: Yes, like me! … Vanessa, could you make me some tea with honey and lemon? I think if I have a hot drink, I'll feel a little better.
Vanessa: Sorry, Jake, I have to go.
Jake: Where are you going?
Vanessa: To my yoga class. You should come and try it.
Jake: Yoga? I don't think that's my thing. Just thinking about it gives me a backache!

Unit 16 Adventures in language
CD 1, Track 24 (*British*)
Julia: Excuse me, Mrs Bell, do you have a minute?
Teacher: Of course, Julia. How can I help you?
Julia: Well, I want to improve my English and I'm not sure what to do. What's the best way to learn English properly?
Teacher: Well, I'm afraid there's no one way to learn a language. All learners are different and learn in different ways. What do you like doing? Do you like writing?
Julia: Yes, I do. I think it's easier to learn things if I write them down.

Teacher: Hmm. Well, for example, you can try and write sentences with words you have learned in class. You can also send emails and messages in English to your friends. But you need to practise speaking a bit more, too. You're very quiet in class.
Julia: Yes, because I'm worried about grammar mistakes.
Teacher: Grammar mistakes don't matter if people understand you. It's better to speak more and practise pronouncing the words. You don't have to have a perfect English accent.
Julia: My parents would like me to do an English course in the summer. Is that a good idea?
Teacher: Yes, it's a very good idea. There are lots of good schools in the UK but you can also learn English in other English-speaking countries like America, Australia, or even Malta, where there are lots of language schools.
Julia: Yes, I've looked on the internet, but there are thousands of courses. How can I find a good one?
Teacher: Well, why don't you come and see me later in the week? Make a list of what exactly you want to do, and I can help you find a course.
Julia: That would be great, thanks.
Teacher: On Friday I'm going to a concert, but I'm free on Thursday after school.
Julia: I'm afraid I'm playing basketball after school on Thursday. What about lunchtime?
Teacher: Er, Thursday lunchtime … yes, that's OK. Would one o'clock suit you?
Julia: Yes, that's fine. Thanks.
Teacher: Right, see you then, Julia.

Unit 16 Adventures in language
CD 1, Track 25 (*British*)
Pronunciation: Intonation in questions
(*See workbook page 37*)
A Listen to these questions from the listening activity 5 in Unit 16. Does the speaker's voice rise or fall?
   1 What's the best way to learn English?
   2 What do you like doing?
   3 How can I find a good course?
   4 Why don't you come and see me later in the week?
B Now listen to these questions. Does the speaker's voice rise or fall?
   1 Do you have a minute?
   2 Do you like writing?
   3 Is that a good idea?
   4 Would one o'clock suit you?

Units 1–3 Word list

Key:
Student Book Page 18
Workbook Unit Wu06
Listening Unit Au12

Unit 1
Adrenalin rush, 8-11

admire, to, 8
adrenalin rush, 8
ambulance, 11
argument, 10
athlete, 9
avoid, to, 9
ball, Wu01
bandage, 11
baseball, 8
BMX bike, 8
bone, 8
boring, 8
breath, Au01
broken, 8
bruise, 8
bungee jumping, 8
coach, 11
cold, Wu01
column, 10
compete, 9
compress, 11
crack, 8
crazy, Au01
cushion, 11
cut, 8
danger, 8
don't panic, 11
elevate, 11
emergency services, 11
exercise, Au01
extreme sports, 8
feeling, 9
field, Au01
First Aid, 11
football (UK),
   soccer (US), 8
goggles, Au01
guard (wrist), 11
helmet, Au01
hobby, 8
hospital, 8
hurt, to, 8
ice, 11
injury, Wu01
inline skates, 8
instructor, Au01
jump, 9
knee, 8
land, to, Wu01
lie down, to, 11
memory, Wu01
mobile phone, 11
motocross, Wu01
pad (knee), 11
parachute, Au01
persuade, to, 9
protect, to, 10
protective suit, Au01
relax, to, 8
rest, to, 11
rib, 8
rider, Wu01
roller skates, 9
routine, 9
safe, 8
save up, to, 9
scared, to be, 10
scream, Au01
skydiving, 8
soccer (UK),
   football (UK), 8
sprain, 8
stay off, to, 11
surfboard, Wu01
surfing, 8
swell up, to, 11
swimming, 8
team, 10
tennis, 8
thrilling, 10
tip, a, 11
took off, to, Wu01
tradition, Wu01
water, Wu01
wave, 9
wheel, Wu01
worried, 8
wrist, 8

Unit 2
Carnival atmosphere, 12-15

AIDS, 13
alcohol, 14
amp, Wu02
atmosphere, 13
band, 15
beat, the, 15
cable, Wu02
Calypso music, Au02
Caribbean, Au02
carnival, 12
Catholic, 13
CD, 15
celebrate, to, 12
censor, 13
Christian, 13
club, 15
coffee plantation, 13
commercial, 13
complain, to, 13
condom, 13
controversial, 12
corrupt, 12
costume, 12
creative, 15
crime, 12
crowd, 14
dance, to, 13
deck, mixing music, 15
decoration, 12
DJ, 15
drugs, 12
drunk, Au02
Easter, 13
enthusiasm, 13
event, 14
everywhere, 14
feather, 12
festival, 12
flag, 12
float, 12
group, Wu02
headphones, Wu02
hip hop music, Au02
image, 14
jazz, Au02
knives, Au02
Lent, 13
mix (music), 15
multicultural, 12
music technology, 15
musical instrument, 15
needle (on turntable), 15
organiser, 14
parade, 12
passionately, 13
police officer, Au02
protest, to make a, 12
proud, 13
Reggae, Au02
reporter, 14
rhythm, 15
safe sex, 13
samba school, 13
Sambódromo, 12
scratch (music), 15
singer, 15
slave, 12
social club, 13
song, 15
Soul (music), Au02
sound system, Au02
speaker (loudspeaker),
   Wu02
spoil, to, 14
sponsorship, 12
steel band, Au02
support, 12
take over, to, 13
team, 12
television rights, 13
theme, 12
tired, Wu02
tourism, 13
track (music), 15
turntable, 15
version, 15
vinyl disc, 15
violence, 14
vocal (music), 15

Unit 3
Lifestyle choices, 16-19

accident, Au03
account executive, 19
accountant, 19
adventure, 18
advertisement, 19
advertising agency, 19
agenda, 19
Alps, Wu03
bank, Au03
boring, Au03
boss, 16
brainstorm, 19
business, 16
career adviser, 18
chairperson, 19
challenging, 16
choice, 18
circle, 19
cleaner, 17
company (a business)
   16
computer programmer,
   16
conclude, 17
creative, 19
dangerous, Au03
decision-making, 19
democratic, 19
disaster, Au03
employee, Wu03
environment, Wu03
financial analyst, 18
financial records, 16
flat (UK),
   apartment (US), 17
flip chart, 19
freelance, 18
friendly, 17

Word list

Units 3–5

garden centre, 17
geek, 18
goal (aim), Wu03
happy, 17
healthy, 17
hotel, Wu03
ICT / IT, 19
information, 19
interesting, Wu03
job satisfaction, 19
lifestyle, 16
manager, 16
managing director, 19
marketing consultant, 19
maths, Au03
media, Au03
meeting, 16
minutes, the, 19
motivate, 19
off track, to go, 19
office, Au03
organise, to, 19
outdoors, 18
partnership, 16
photographer, Au03
place, 19
plants (growing), 16
presentation (business), 19
promotion (career), 18
reception (hotel), 17
reporter, 18
risky, Wu03
routine, 18
run (a company), to 16
salary, 18
sales manager, 19
secure, to be, 16
set up, to, 16
sheep, Wu03
ship, Wu03
software, 16
sole trader, 16
specialist, 16
stressful, 16
techie, 18
technology, Au03
training, 19
travel, 18
U-shape, 19
variety, 18
wasted, to be, 19
web designer, 19
winter sports, 16
work for themselves, 16
working with people, 17
your own boss, to be, 16

Unit 4
Stranger than fiction, 20-23

actor, 23
appearance, Au04
aunt, 22
beauty queen, 22
best friend, 22
blind date, Au04
body, 21
brave, Au04
breast (operation), 21
cast (of a film), 23
celebrity, 20
challenge (on reality TV), 20
character (in a TV show), 22
complicated, 23
contestant, 20
continuity (in movies), 23
cope, to, 22
cousin, 22
crew (film), 23
critic, 20
daughter, 22
definitely, 22
documentary, 20
dumb (US), 22
entertainment, 20
error, 23
exploit, to, 21
fantasy, 23
fault (their own), 22
fiction, 20
film (UK), movie (US), 23
film, to, 23
game park, Au04
game show, 20
gross (US), 20
harmless, 20
hot coals (walking over), 21
humiliate, 22
influence, to, 23
island, 21
judges, Au04
light (for filming), 23
location, 23
make up (cosmetics), 20
make-over (TV show), 23
media studies, 23
mirror, Au04
mistakes, 23
mom (US), 22
movie (US), 23
neighbour, 22
old-fashioned, 21

operation (plastic surgery), 21
order (of shots), 23
organisation, an, 20
painful, Au04
patient (medical), 21
plastic surgery, 20
plot (of film), 23
popular, 21
presenter (of a TV show), 22
prize, 20
producer (film), 20
programme (TV), 20
rat, 21
reality, 21
review (of TV), 20
scene, 23
schedule (shooting), 23
science fiction, 23
series (TV), 20
shoot (a film), 23
show (TV), 21
sister, 22
soap opera, 20
spiders, 20
stomach, 21
studio, 23
stupid, Au04
summarise, 21
talk show, 20
the news, 20
the old man of (reality TV), 21
they suck! (US), 22
throat, Au04
timetable, 23
trend, 21
trivialise, to, 21
tropical, 21
TV show, 20
unattractive, 22
viewer, 20
visual, 23
vocal chords, Au04
vote, to, 21
weather, 23
windows, 23
worm, 22

Unit 5
Shopaholics, 24-27

account (store card account), 25
afford, to, 25
angry, anger, Wu05
backpack, 24
bargain, 25

birthday present, Au05
camera, 26
cancel, to, 27
cash, 24
cheque (UK), check (US), 24
complain, to, Wu05
complaint (to a shop), 24
confirmation (of your order), 27
connected with, 24
consumer rights, 27
correct (adj), Au05
countable nouns, Wu05
credit card, 24
credit card statement, 27
credit note, 26
criticise, to, 25
customer, 24
customer service, 24
delivery, Au05
discount, 25
down, to be or feel, 25
electronics, 24
exchange, to, 26
expensive, 25
experience (shopping), 25
explain, to, Wu05
faulty (goods), 24
gift, Au05
good buy (or bad buy), 26
goods, 24
handbag (UK), purse (US), 24
hate, to, 25
horrible, 25
image, 25
interest (money percentage), 25
item, 26
lunch break, Au05
manager, Au05
method (sales), 24
mosquito, 25
newsagent, 24
online, 27
padlock (symbol), 27
personal information, 27
point of view, 25
polite, 26
postal address, 27
pressure (to put on them), 25
pressurise, to, 25
privacy statement, 27
products, 27
proof, 27
purse (UK), wallet (US), 24

Units 5–7 Word list

pushy (sales assistants), 24
receipt (in a shop), 24
recommend, Au05
refund, 24
repel, to, 25
right now, Au05
rip-off, a, 24
rude, 25
sale (money off), 24
sales assistant, 24
sales method, 24
services, 27
shocking, Wu05
shopaholic, 24
shopping centre, 26
shout, to, 26
silly, 25
spend, to, 27
store (credit) card, 24
stuff, Wu05
suit, to (clothes suit you), 25
target, 25
wallet (UK), billfold (US), 24
weekend, 26
workplace, 25
written proof, 27
wrong (with it), 27

Unit 6
Eat your greens! 28-31

accident, Wu06
advantage, 30
angry, 30
argument, 30
aubergine (UK), eggplant (US), Wu06
beans, 31
bland, 28
boring, 30
BSE (mad cow disease), 29
busy, Wu06
Caesar salad, 30
café, 30
calorie, 31
carrot, Wu06
category (of foods), 31
cereal, 31
cheese, 31
chemicals (in food), 29
chicken, Wu06
condition (of your body), 29
contribute, to, 29
crocodile, Wu06

crops, Au06
cruel, 30
daily, 31
dairy produce, 28
decrease (noun), Wu06
decrease, to, Wu06
delicious, 28
dessert, 30
diet (noun), 31
disgusting, 28
dog, Wu06
eat out, to, Wu06
economy, Wu06
eggs, 29
environment, Wu06
export (noun), Wu06
export, to, Wu06
fantastic, 28
farmer, Au06
fat, 31
fish, 28
fries (US), chips (UK), 30
fruit, 28
genes, 30
global warming, 28
GM (genetically modified) food, 30
greens (vegetables), 28
group (of foods), 31
healthy, 28
heart disease, 28
heavy (a person), 31
honey, 29
horrible, 28
hungry, 29
ideal, Wu06
industry association, 30
iron (in a diet), 30
kangaroo, Wu06
lamb, 28
leather, 28
lettuce, 28
livestock, 28
meal, Wu06
measurement, 31
mention, to, 30
menu, Wu06
methane, 28
milk, 28
miserable, 29
mouthwatering, 28
noisy, Wu06
nutrient, 28
nuts, 31
oil (food), 31
orange, 28
overweight, Wu06
pasta, 31

potato, Wu06
poultry, 31
produce (noun), Wu06
produce, to, Wu06
pyramid, 31
rainforest, 29
region, 28
research (noun), 29
research, to, 28
restaurant, 30
rice, 31
salmon, 28
saturated fat, 31
serving (portion), 31
soil, 28
sparingly, 31
sweets, 31
taste (noun), 28
taste, to, 30
tasty, 28
tea, Wu06
thin, Au06
thirsty, 29
tomato, Au06
unhealthy, 28
vegan, 29
vegetable, 28
vegetarian, 28
vegetarianism, 29
vitamins, 30
waste, to, 28
weight (person), 31
yoghurt, 31

Unit 7
For your eyes only, 32-35

access (noun), 32
angry, 32
attention-getter, 35
awful, 33
blog, 32
blogger, 32
bomb (noun), 33
brainstorm, 35
bullet points, 35
calm, 32
chat, 32
chat room, 34
clean your teeth, 32
clever, Wu07
complete, 33
computer, 34
control, Au07
course (school, computer), Wu07
creative writing, 35
cry, to, 32

dance, to, 32
decision, 33
depressed, 32
desk, Wu07
diary, 33
editor, 32
emphasise, Wu07
excited, 32
feel sure, 32
feelings, 32
fly, to, Wu07
full-time, Wu07
give me a break, Au07
happy, 32
hates (group of hates), 33
imaginary (event), Wu07
in private, Wu07
in public, Wu07
interest (hobbies), 33
internet, 34
journalist, 33
keep private, to, 32
lonely, 32
loves (his loves are...), 33
nerd, 34
news, 33
online, 33
outline (of an essay), 35
personal experience, 33
piece (of writing), 35
post, to (as in website), 32
private, 32
professional, 33
properly, 34
propose (marriage), 33
proud, 32
public place, 34
publish, to, 33
real (event), Wu07
relationship, 34
relieved (to feel), 32
remain calm, 32
revise, 35
romantic, 33
rubbish, 34
sad, 32
scared, 32
secret, 33
self-centered, 34
self-confidence, 32
self-control, 32
self-exposure, 32
self-help, 32
share, to, 33
shout, 33
skill (writing), 35
smart (intelligent), Au07
spell, to, Au07

Word list

Units 7–9

spot, to, 35
stranger, 33
thought, 33
tip (hint), 35
trip (journey), Wu07
upset, 32
war, 33
web (internet), 34

Unit 8
Fashionistas, 36-39

accessories (fashion), 36
ask (someone) out, Au08
bag (handbag), 36
baggy, 36
beep (noise of phone), 38
blouse, 37
boots, 37
bracelet, 36
call me back, Au08
capital (city), Wu08
casual, 36
chat, 38
cheap, 37
checked (pattern), 36
chemicals (in farming), 39
clothing, 36
colour, 37
comfortable, 36
consumer, 36
cool, 36
cotton, 37
country-style, 37
creative, 37
customer, 38
dangerous, 39
date (to date someone), 38
designer (adj as in suit), 37
dishonest, Wu08
dislike, Wu08
download, Au08
dress, a, 37
dump, to (dump a friend), 38
dye (to dye hair), 37
earrings, 36
eco (eco-friendly), 37
electronics (goods), 36
environment, 39
ethnic, 37
expensive, 37
exploit, to, 39
express, to, 36
eye-catching, 36
factory, 39
fair trade, 39
fashion, 36
fashion slave, 37

fashionista, 37
fit, to (clothes), 38
flamboyant, 36
footwear, Wu08
formal, 36
globalisation, 39
gold, 37
Gothic, 37
hair, 37
harm, to, 39
hat, 36
haute couture (fashion), Wu08
head to toe, 37
headscarf, 37
hip-hop, 37
horrible, Au08
imperfect, Wu08
in look, 37
indefinite, Wu08
individual, 37
item, 36
jacket, Wu08
jeans, Wu08
jewellery, 36
khaki, 37
leader, 36
loose (clothes), 36
luxury, 36
matching, 37
meet, to, 38
military, 37
model (fashion model), Wu08
necklace, 36
notice, to, Wu08
organic, 37
organised, Wu08
out of it (excluded), Au08
outerwear, Wu08
patterned, 36
personality, 36
plain, 36
polite, Wu08
pollution, 39
professional, 37
punk (band), Wu08
relaxed, 36
rich (noun, the), 37
role model, 37
running shoes, 37
sandals, 37
scarf, 36
second-hand, 37
seeing someone (dating), Au08
shirt, 37
smart, 36

socks, 37
special, 37
sportswear, Wu08
spotted, 36
street fashion, 36
striped, stripe, 36
style, 37
suit (men's suit), 37
sunglasses, 36
supplier, 39
survey, Au08
sustainable (clothing), 39
text (message), 38
tidy, 36
tight (clothes), Wu08
trainers (shoes), Wu08
trend, 36
trousers (pair of), 39
T-shirt, 39
uncool, Wu08
underwear, 37
unique, Wu08
watch, a (timepiece), 36
wear, to, 36
well-dressed, 36
wooden, 37
workers (in factory), 39

Extended reading 1, 40-41

apply to, 40
at sea, 40
aunt, 40
average, 40
boat, 40
bother, to, 41
boyfriend, 41
break a record, to, 40
bucket, 40
computer, 41
cook, (noun), 41
dangerous, 40
deep-sea (sport), 41
diary, 41
differ, to, 41
doctor, 41
expanse, 40
experience, 40
expert, 42
extraordinary, 40
fame, 40
family, 41
feelings, 40
freeze-dried, 41
give a face to, 41
hard disc, 41
iceberg, 41
injury, 41

interview (give an...), 41
latest, 40
live off, 41
lonely, 40
luxury, 40
mechanic, 41
meteorologist, 40
miss, to (lack), 40
nap (sleep), 40
navigator, 41
ocean, 41
on board, 41
plan, a, 41
practical side, 40
race, 40
rain, 41
relaxing, 40
respect (in every), 41
rhythm, 41
sail, a, 41
sail, to, 40
ship, 41
shower, a (wash in), 40
smell, to, 41
solo, 40
soul, 40
sport, 41
stuff (that stuff), 41
success, 40
survival, 40
take a chance, 41
technology, 40
thought (noun), 40
treat, to, 41
voyage, 40
warm, 40
wash, to, 40
weather, 41
webcam, 41

Unit 9
Rule of law, 42-45

against the law, 42
alcohol, 42
allowed, 42
angry, 43
arrest, 42
art form, Wu09
author, Au09
ban, to, 44
border, 45
break the law, Wu09
chair, 43
childhood, 43
cinema, Wu09
citizen, 45
citizenship, 45
clean up, Au09

Units 9–10 Word list

coffee, Wu09
collect, to, 43
commit a crime, 42
commune, a, 42
control, to, 44
convenient, Au09
Council of the European Union, 45
cousin, Wu09
crime, 43
criminal, 42
Customs, 45
dance, 43
decision, 44
defend, to, 43
dentist, 43
develop, to, 42
drink (alcohol), 43
drop, to, 42
dye, to (clothes), 43
economic union, 45
EU (European Union), 45
EU member states, 45
Euro €, 45
European Commission, 45
European Parliament, 45
follower, 43
fraud, 42
free (to be), 43
freedom, 44
give up, 42
going a bit far, Au09
gold teeth, 44
government control, Au09
graffiti, 42
guru, 43
hair gel, 44
identity, 45
illegal, 42
individual, 44
kids (children), 43
kiss goodnight, 43
law (noun), 42
legal, 44
Lego, 43
library, Wu09
litter, 42
lonely, 43
mayor, Au09
meditate, to, 43
mistake, 44
motto, 45
murder, 42
museum, Wu09
national, 45
necessity, 43

need to, 43
obey, to, 42
obligation, 43
passport control, 45
perfume, 44
personality, 43
pigeon, 44
plastic bag, Wu09
political union, 45
pollution, Wu09
possession, 42
prison, 42
programme (radio), Au09
propose, to (new laws), 45
public place, Au09
radio, 44
receipt, Wu09
regulations, 42
restaurant, Wu09
restriction, 42
risk, to, 42
rule of law, 45
share, to, 42
shoplift, 42
shower, Wu09
sing, 43
single market, 45
smell (noun), Au09
smoke, to (tobacco), 42
social behaviour, 44
survey, 42
tax, Wu09
teenage, 43
ticket, Wu09
toilet, Wu09
tooth, teeth, Au09
trade, 45
unusual, 43
white, Au09

Unit 10
What's next?
46-49

anger, 47
appliance, 48
battery, Wu10
body language, 49
brain, 49
button, 46
cable, 46
camera, 49
century, 46
communicate, to, 49
computer, 49
conduct, to (an orchestra), 49
connect, to, Wu10
contact lens, Wu10

dark, 46
data, 49
day, 46
decade, 46
development (noun), 46
digital camera, Wu10
disaster, Au10
discover, to, Wu10
dishwasher, Au10
DNA, 49
dream, 47
drive (hard disk drive), Wu10
DVD player, 46
environment (friendly), 47
experiment, an, 46
factory, 47
fear, 47
feelings, 47
fit in, to, 47
flat screen (TV), 48
founder, 46
fridge, 47
friendly, 47
futurist, Wu10
gadget, Wu10
gasped, 47
general (adj), Wu10
go wrong, to, Au10
ground-breaking, 47
hardware, 49
hour, 46
household, 48
housework, 47
IBM (company), 46
ignorant, 47
inform, to, Wu10
information technology (IT), 49
instruction manual, Au10
instructions, 46
intelligent, Wu10
invent, to, 46
invention, 46
laboratory, a, 46
light, 46
live without, to, 46
living standard, Wu10
love, 47
machine, 48
magic, 47
microphone, 49
minute, 46
mistake, Au10
monitor (computer screen), Au10

month, 46
old-fashioned, 47
optimistic, 49
outside world, 47
personality, 49
pessimistic, Wu10
physical activity, 49
physical world, 47
plug in, to, 46
population, 48
precisely, 47
predict, to, Wu10
prediction, 47
press, to, 46
printer (computer printer), Wu10
printing press, 46
process, to (information), 49
product, Wu10
program (computer), 49
programmer, 49
progress (noun), 48
puzzled, to be, 47
reason, to, 47
recognise, to, 49
right and wrong, 47
robot, 46
robotics, 49
science fiction, 47
scientific, 46
screen, Wu10
social changes, Wu10
socket, 46
software, 49
solution, Wu10
solve, to, 46
space (alone in), Wu10
switch (noun), 46
switch, to (on / off), 46
task, a, 49
technological, 46
technology, 47
telephone, 46
test, to, 46
the future, 46
think for itself, to, 47
twentieth century, 47
uncomfortable, 47
upstairs, 47
USB port, Wu10
vacuum cleaner, 48
video, Au10
voice, 49
washing machine, 48
wheel, 46
wireless technology, Wu10

Word list

Unit 11
Travel costs, 50-53

air pollution, Wu11
air travel, 50
airline, 50
airport, 51
airport tax, Au11
bike, Wu11
biology, 53
boat, 50
book, to, 51
boss, a (your boss), 52
breathe, to, 53
broaden, to, 52
bus, 50
calculate, to, 52
car, 50
carbon dioxide (CO2), 51
celebrity, a, 52
cell, a (plant), 53
Channel Tunnel, Wu11
charger, a (phone charger), 52
cheap, 50
climate change , 50
connect, to, Wu11
convenient, inconvenient, 50
crowd, a, 53
damage, 51
dangerous, 50
desert, Wu11
diagram, 53
disadvantage, 53
double, 50
duration, 53
eco-friendly, 50
energy, 52
environment, the, 50
environmentalists, 51
expensive, 50
fare, a, 50
ferry, 50
flight, a, 50
fuel, 50
gas, 53
global warming, 51
glucose, 53
heart problem, 51
holiday, Wu11
horseriding, Wu11
hybrid (electric / petrol) car, 50
I'm not with you, 52
journey, 50
jumbo jet, 50
Kyoto climate conference / Kyoto Protocol, Wu11
leaf, 53
luxury, 50
motorbike, Wu11
noise, 51
on foot, 50
online, 51
overcrowded, 51
oxygen, 53
passenger, 50
photosynthesis, 53
plane, 50
plant, to (trees), 52
pollute, to, 50
programme (tree-planting), 52
quick, 50
relaxing, 50
report, a, 51
respiration, 53
root, 53
safe, 50
sail, to, Wu11
scary, Au11
slow, 50
So what? 52
speed, 53
stress, 51
sugar, 53
sunlight, 53
talking point, Wu11
tax, 50
traffic, 50
train, Au11
trip (noun), 52
visit, to, Wu11
website, Au11
weekend, Au11
World Health Organisation (WHO), 51
worth, 51

Unit 12
Money, money, money, 54-57

account (bank), 54
amazed, 55
arrangement, Wu12
art (noun, work of), 56
audio, Au12
balance (bank), 54
bank account, 56
banking, 54
banknote, 57
beg, to, 54
behaviour, 56
book, to, 55
borrow, 54
careful, 55
cash, 55
cashpoint / ATM, 54
chance (noun), 55
change (noun, money), Wu12
cheat, to, Wu12
checkout assistant, 56
close down, to, Wu12
coin, 54
company (firm), 54
credit card, Wu12
crime, 55
criminal, 55
currency, 57
current (adj, now), 57
customer, 55
dishonest, 56
earn, to, 54
Euro (€), 57
exchange rate, 57
fault, 55
faulty (machine), 55
foreign exchange (Forex), 57
generous, Wu12
holiday, 55
homework, 56
honest, 54
hurt, to, 55
internet banking, 54
invest, to, 54
investor, 56
it is unlikely that, 57
lazy, Wu12
lottery, 54
lucky, 55
machine, 55
maths (UK), math (US), 56
millions (money), Au12
mistake, 55
neighbour, 55
note (money), 54
opening hours, Wu12
part-time, 56
pin number, 54
politician, 56
pound (£), 57
prison, 55
quality, a (personal), 54
queue, to, 55
quiz, Au12
replace, 57
resist, to, 55
responsible, to be, 55
rich, 56
save, to, 54
schoolboy, 55
security company, 55
serious, 55
shares (in a company), Wu12
sofa, 55
software, 55
something for nothing, 55
sooner or later, Au12
spend, to, 54
steal, to, 54
supermarket, 56
survey, 54
sweetshop, 55
US dollar ($), 57
value, 57
wallet, 56
weak currency, 57
win, to, 54
yen (¥), 57

Unit 13
Destination disaster, 58-61

accelerate, to, 58
accident, 59
aggressive, 59
altitude, 61
angry, 59
annoy, to, 59
anti-car group, 60
argument, 60
attack (noun), 59
audio, Au13
backpack, Wu13
bag, Wu13
bicycle, 58
brake, 58
break, to (speed record), 61
campaign, 60
car park, 60
commit, to, 59
contribute, to, 59
cool (adj, fashionable), 58
cool (temperature), 61
crash, to, 58
cycle lane, Wu13
cyclist, 59
dangerous, 59
death, 59
doctor, Au13
drive, to, 58
driver, 59
driving test, 59
encourage, to, 60
exhaust pipe, 58

Units 13–14 Word list

explosion, 61
express, to, Wu13
fantastic, Wu13
fast, 58
football match, Au13
freedom, Au13
freeway (US), motorway (UK), 59
frighten, to, 59
garage (parking), Au13
girlfriend, 60
go past, to, 58
group (organisation), Au13
handlebars, 58
harm, to, 59
healthy, 60
height, 61
helmet, 59
impress, to, Wu13
in order to, Wu13
incident, 59
independent, Wu13
inexperienced, Wu13
injure, to, 59
internet, Wu13
junction, 58
land speed record, 61
local, Wu13
loud, Au13
military-style, 59
motorway (UK), freeway (US), 58
movement, 61
music, Au13
newsagent, Wu13
newspaper, Wu13
organisation, Au13
overtake, to, 58
park, 58
parking space, 59
part-time job, Wu13
pedal, 58
pensioner, 59
personality, 61
petrol station, Au13
physics, 61
plan, to, Wu13
pro-car group, Wu13
quick, 60
radio, 60
record, a (speed record), 61
red, Wu13
road rage, 59
roundabout (UK), traffic circle (US), 58
rubbish, Au13

saddle, 58
safe, 58
scary, 59
sea level, 61
secretary, 59
shockwave, 61
shoot, to, 59
silly, Au13
smell, 61
sonic boom, 61
sound wave, 61
space (area), Au13
speed, 58
speed limit, 59
speed of sound, 61
sports utility vehicle (SUV), 59
station (train), Wu13
steering wheel, 58
sticker, 59
street, 61
stress, 59
supersonic, 61
take up, to, 59
technology, 59
temperature, 61
tiny, Wu13
traffic jam, 58
traffic lights, 58
transport, to, Au13
uncle, Wu13
uncomfortable, Wu13
vehicle, 58
view (noun, my view), Wu13
weapon, 59
wear, to, 59
weather, 59
wheel, 58
windscreen, Wu13

Unit 14
All in the family, 62-65

aisle, 63
anniversary, 62
argument, 65
beach, 63
best man, Au14
bikini, 63
birth, 62
birthday, 62
book, to, 63
boyfriend, 64
bridesmaid, 62
brother, 62
card (greetings), 62
celebrate, to, 62

certificate, Wu14
childless, 65
church, 63
cleaning (household), Au14
clothes, 63
clubbing, Au14
colleague, 65
congratulations, Au14
conversation, 64
cooking, the, 64
couple, 63
cricket ground, 63
cry, to, 63
custom, 65
dance, to, 63
decorating, 64
dinner, Au14
disco, 63
divorce, 62
DJ, 63
document, 62
dress, a, 63
educate, to, 65
enjoy, 63
extended family, 65
fall asleep, Wu14
fall over, Wu14
family member, 62
father, 62
five-course meal, 63
flat (UK), apartment (US), Au14
formal, 62
full-time job, Au14
function, a, 65
generation, 65
get engaged, to, 62
get married, 62
girlfriend, 64
graduation, 62
grandparent, 65
guest, Wu14
half-sister, 62
happiness, 62
hell, 62
holiday, 62
honeymoon, 62
hotel, 63
household job, 64
housework, 64
husband, 62
I do (as in wedding), 63
ironing, the, Wu14
job, 65
lazy, Au14
lie, to (lie down), Wu14
life event, 62

live together (cohabit), 63
marriage, 62
marry, to, 62
Mediterranean, Wu14
mother, 65
nervous, Wu14
normal, 63
nowadays, Au14
nuclear family, 65
occasion, 62
old people, 65
online, 63
only child, 62
painting, Au14
parents, 62
partner, 62
penfriend, Wu14
preparation, 64
private, 63
reception, 62
relative (relations), 65
romantic, 63
save up, to, Wu14
shine, to (sun), 63
shopping, Au14
sign, to, 62
silver wedding, Au14
single parent, 62
sister, 62
situation, 64
skydiving, 63
slave, Au14
social group, 65
society, 65
speech, 63
stadium, 63
stage (on), Wu14
stepfamily, 65
stepfather, 62
stress, 62
Thank goodness! Au14
the big day, 63
traditional, 63
typical, 65
underwater, 63
unpaid, Au14
waitress, 63
washing, the, 64
wave, to, Wu14
wear, to (clothes), 64
weather, 64
wedding, 62
wedding planner, 63
West, the 65
white wedding, 63
wife, Wu14
witness, 62